ESTO PERPETUA

ESTO PERPETUA
ALGERIAN STUDIES AND IM-
PRESSIONS BY H. BELLOC

AMS PRESS
NEW YORK

Reprinted from the edition of 1906, London
First AMS EDITION published 1969
Manufactured in the United States of America

Library of Congress Catalogue Card Number: 79-95146

AMS PRESS, INC.
NEW YORK, N. Y. 10003

TO

E. S. P. HAYNES

INTRODUCTION

☦ ONCE, in a village that overlooked the Mediterranean, I saw a man working in an open shop, fitting together a builder's Ornament which was to go upon the ridge-end of some roof or other. He was making the base of the Ornament so as to fit on to a certain angle of the rafters, and the Ornament itself was a Cross. It was spring-time, and he was singing.

I asked him for whom he was making it. He answered, for a man who had ordered it of him over-sea in Algiers.

But another Ornament also stood by, carved in the same way, and similar in size. I asked him for whom he had

INTRODUCTION

finished that other, and he said, "For the same man over-sea: he puts them upon buildings." This second Ornament, however, happened to be a Crescent.

The contrast moved me to cross the sea, to understand the land upon the further shore, and to write upon Africa some such little historical essay as follows.

When a man first sees Africa, if it is just before the rising of the sun, he perceives, right up against a clean horizon, what appear to be islands standing out distinct and sharp above the sea.

At this hour a wind is often blowing from the eastward, and awakens the Mediterranean as though it came purposely at dawn to make the world ready for the morning. The little waves leap up beneath it, steep towards their shadows, and the bows of the ship that had surged all night through a rolling calm begin, as sailors say, to

The Landfall

"speak": the broken water claps and babbles along the side. In this way, if he has good fortune, the traveller comes upon a new land. It is that land, shut off from all the rest between the desert and the sea, which the Arabs call the Island of the West, the Maghreb, but to which we in Europe for many hundred years have given the name of Barbary: as it says in the song about freedom:

> ". . . as large as a Lion reclined
> By the rivers of Barbary."

It is the shore that runs, all built upon a single plan, from Tunis and the Gulf of Carthage to Tangier; that was snatched from Europe in one great cavalry charge twelve hundred years ago, and is now at last again in the grasp of Europe.

For many hours the traveller will sail towards it until at last he comes to a belt of smooth water which, in such weather, fringes all that coast, and then he finds

The Roads

that what he saw at morning was not a line of islands, but the tops of high hills standing in a range along the sea: they show darker against a stronger light and a more southerly sun as he draws nearer, and beyond them he sees far off inland the first buttress mountains which hold up the plateaux of Atlas.

The country which he thus approaches differs in its fortune and history from all others in the world. The soil and the relief of the Maghreb, coupled with its story, have made it peculiar and, as it were, a symbol of the adventures of Europe. Ever since our western race began its own life and entered into its ceaseless struggle against the East, this great bastion has been held and lost again; occupied by our enemies and then taken back as our power re-arose.

The Character

The Phœnician ruled it; Rome wrested it back; it fell for the last time when the Roman Empire declined; its reconquest has been the latest fruit of our recovery.

It is thoroughly our own. The race that has inhabited it from its origin and still inhabits it is our race; its climate and situation are ours; it is at the furthest limit from Asia; it is an opposing shore of our inland sea; it links Sicily to Spain; it retains in every part of it the Menhirs and the Dolmens, the great stones at which our people sacrificed when they began to be men: yet even in the few centuries of written history foreign gods have twice been worshipped there and foreign rulers have twice held it for such long spaces of time that twice its nature has been forgotten. Even to-day, when our reoccupation seems assured, we speak of it as though it were by some right originally Oriental, and by some destiny certain to remain so. During the many centuries of our decline and of our slow resurrection, these countries were first cut off so suddenly and so clean from Christendom, next steeped so long and so thoroughly in an alien religion and habit of law, that their very dress and language changed; and until a man has recognised at last the faces beneath the turbans, and has seen and grown familiar with the great buildings which Rome nowhere founded more solidly than in these provinces, he is deceived by the tradition of an immediate past and by the externals of things: he sees nothing but Arabs around him, and feels himself an intruder from a foreign world.

Of this eastern spirit, which is still by far the strongest to be found in the states of Barbary, an influence meets one long before one has made land. The little ships all up and down the Mediterranean, and especially as one nears the African coast, are in their rig and their whole manner Arabian.

The Normal Sail

There is a sort of sail which may be called the original of all sails. It is the sail with which antiquity was familiar. It brought the ships to Tenedos and the Argo carried it. The Norwegians had it when they were pirates a thousand years ago. They have it still. It is nearer a lug-sail than anything else, and indeed our Deal luggers carry something very near it. It is almost a square sail, but the yard has a slight rake and there is a bit of a peak to it. It is the kind of sail which seems to come first into the mind of any man when he sets out to use the wind. It is to be seen continually to-day hoisted above small boats in the north of Europe.

But this sail is too simple. It will not go close to the wind, and in those light and variable airs which somehow

The Lateen

have no force along the deck, it hangs empty and makes no way because it has no height.

Now when during that great renaissance of theirs in the seventh century the Arabs left their deserts and took to the sea, they became for a short time in sailing, as in philosophy, the teachers of their new subjects. They took this sail which they had found in all the ports they had conquered along this coast — in Alexandria, in Cyrene, in Carthage, in Cæsarea — they lightened and lengthened the yard, they lifted the peak up high, they clewed down the foot, and very soon they had that triangular *lateen* sail which will, perhaps, remain when every other evidence of their early conquering energy has disappeared. With such a sail they drove those first fleets of theirs which gave them at once the islands and the commerce of the Mediterranean. It was the sail which permitted

The Lateen

their invasion of the northern shores and the unhappy subjection of Spain.

We Europeans have for now some seven hundred years, from at least the Third Crusade, so constantly used this gift of Islam that we half forget its origin. You may see it in all the Christian harbours of the Mediterranean to-day, in every port of the Portuguese coast, and here and there as far north as the Channel. It is not to be seen beyond Cherbourg, but in Cherbourg it is quite common. The harbour-boats that run between the fleet and the shore hoist these lateens. Yet it is not of our own making, and, indeed, it bears a foreign mark which is very distinct, and which puzzles every northerner when first he comes across this sail : it reefs along the yard. Why it should do so neither history nor the men that handle it can explain, since single sails are manifestly made to reef from the foot to the leach,

Its Reefing

where a man can best get at them. Not so the lateen. If you carry too much canvas and the wind is pressing her you must take it in from aloft, or, it must be supposed, lower the whole on deck. And this foreign, quaint, unusual thing which stamps the lateen everywhere is best seen when the sail is put away in harbour. It does not lie down along the deck as do ours in the north, but right up along the yard, and the yard  itself is kept high at the masthead, making a great bow across the sky, and (one would say) tempting Providence to send a gale and wreck it. Save for this mark—which may have its uses, but seems to have none and to be merely barbaric—the lateen is perfect in its kind, and might be taken with advantage throughout the world (as it is throughout all this united sea) for the

The Little Ships

uniform sail. For this kind of sail is, for small craft, the neatest and the swiftest in the world, and, in a general way, will lie closer to the wind than any other. Our own fore-and-aft rig is nothing else but a lateen cut up into mainsail, foresail, and jib, for the convenience of handling.

The little ships, so rigged, come out like heralds far from the coast to announce the old dominion of the East and of the religion that made them: of the united civilisation that has launched them over all its seas, from east of India to south of Zanzibar and right out here in the western place which we are so painfully recovering. They are the only made thing, the only *form* we accepted from the Arab: and we did well to accept it. The little ships are a delight.

You see them everywhere. They belong to the sea and they animate it. They are similar as waves are similar: they are

The Little Ships

different as waves are different. They come into a hundred positions against the light. They heel and run with every mode of energy.

There is nothing makes a man's heart so buoyant as to see one of the little ships bowling along breast-high towards him, with the wind and the clouds behind it, careering over the sea. It seems to have borrowed something of the air and something of the water, and to unite them both and to be their offspring and also their bond. When they are middle-way over the sea towards one under a good breeze, the little ships are things to remember.

So it is when they carry double sail and go, as we say of our schooners, " wing and wing." For they can carry two sails when

The Little Ships

the wind is moderate, and especially when the vessel is running before it, but these two sails are not carried upon two masts, but both upon the same mast. The one is the common or working sail, carried in all

weathers. The other is a sort of spinnaker, of which you may see the yard lying along decks in harbour or triced up a little by the halyard, so as to swing clear of the hands.

When the little ships come up like this with either sail well out and square and their course laid straight before the general run of a fresh sea, rolling as they go, it is as though the wind had a friend and companion of its own, understanding all its moods, so easily and rapidly do they arrive towards the shore. A little jib (along this coast at least) is bent along the forestay, and the dark line of it marks the swing and movement of the whole. So also when you stand and look from along their wake and see them leaving for the horizon along a slant of the Levantine, with the breeze just on their quarter and their laden hulls careening a trifle to leeward, you would say they were great birds, born of the sea, and sailing down the current from which they were bred. The peaks of their tall sails have a turn to them like the wing-tips of birds, espe- cially of those darting birds which come up to  us from the south after winter and shoot along their way.

Moreover the sails of these little ships never seem to lose the memory of power. Their curves and fulness always suggest a movement of the hull. Very often at sunset when the dead calm reflects things unbroken like an inland pond, the topmost angle of these lateens catches some hesitating air that stirs above, and leads it down the sail, so that a little ripple trembles round the bows of the boat, though all the water beside them is quite smooth, and you see her gliding in without oars. She comes along in front of the twilight, as gradual and as silent as the evening, and seems to be impelled by nothing more substantial than the advance of darkness.

It is with such companions to proclaim the title of the land that one comes round under a point of hills and enters harbour.

* * * * *

To comprehend the accidents which have befallen the Maghreb it is necessary to consider its position and the nature of the boundaries which surround it. In order to

The Mediterranean

do this one must see how it stands with regard to the Mediterranean and to the Desert.

Here is a rough map on which are indicated the shores of that sea, and to appreciate its scale it is easiest to remember

that its whole length from the Straits of Gibraltar at **M** to the Levantine coast at **A** is well over 2000 miles. In this map those shores which are well watered and upon which men can build cities and can live are marked black. The great desert beyond to the south, which perpetually threatens the

The Mediterranean

further shore and in which men can only live here and there in little oases of watered land is marked with sloping lines.

It is easy to see how this great surrounded water nourished the seeds of our civilisation: why all the influences we enjoy here in the north came upwards to us from its harbours: why Asia stretched out towards it in order to learn, and attempted (but always failed) to absorb it. It is so diversified by great peninsulas and very numerous islands that the earliest sailors need never miss the land : it has so indented and varied a coast that harbours are nowhere lacking to it. Its climate is of that kind best suited to men, yielding them fruits and warmth with some labour, but not so hardly as to sour them into brutality nor so cheaply as to degrade them by indolence. The separate homes in which polities can grow up separately and cherish their separate lives, were fortified by the sea which protected its archipelagoes

The Mediterranean

and its long tongues of land, and were further guarded by the many mountain chains which so affect the horizons all along these coasts that almost every landfall you make as you sail is some very high, and often sacred, hill. But all this difference was permitted to interact upon itself and to preserve a common unity by the common presence of the sea. If it be true, as the wisest men have said, that everything comes from salt water, then nowhere in the world could the influence of the sea do more to create and feed the aspirations of men. Whether our race came thither from the north and east, or, as is more probable, from the African shore, this much is certain, that there grew up round the Mediterranean, Europe, which is Ourselves.

At one part things alien to us impinge upon this sea; this part is the eastern bay which is marked off upon the map with a dotted line and the shores of which are the outposts

The Phœnicians

of Asia and of the Egyptians. The projection on the south is that delta of the Nile from which Egypt looked out jealously against rivals whom she despised or ignored: the long Levantine coast which blocks the eastern end of the whole sea was alive with the essence of the Asiatic spirit: with the subtlety, the yielding and the avarice of the Phœnician cities. Egypt may have attempted something westward: there is a legend of struggles with a fair people, and to this day in the salt marshes south of Tunis a group of date-trees, abandoned and unplucked, are called the "Dates of Pharaoh" and resemble no dates of that country, but the dates of the Nile valley. But if such expeditions were made they were fruitless. The desert was still a secure boundary for us: the first attack which Europe was to suffer came not from the sands, but from its own sea, and the first conquerors of the Maghreb were the Phœnicians.

The Phœnicians

This people were Orientals, like any others; but they had, as it were, specialised upon one most notable character of their race, which is to accumulate wealth by negotiation, and to avoid as far as may be the labour of production. To no other family of men has toil appeared to be a curse save to that of which the Phœnicians were members; nor are fatigues tolerable to that family save those endured in acquiring the possessions of others and in levying that toll which cunning can always gather from mere industry. Of all effort travel alone was congenial to them, and especially travel by sea, which, when they had first developed it, became for many centuries their monopoly and gave them the carrying of the world and the arbitrament of its exchanges. They dwelt in a small group of harbours on that extreme eastern shore of the Mediterranean, where a narrow strip of fertile land lay between them and the mountains. They sailed out before the steady northerly and easterly winds of summer, (which are but a portion of the Trade Winds;) they pushed from headland to headland and from island to island, bringing into economic contact the savage tribes and the wealthy states, passionate especially for metals, but carefully arranging that there should arise between the nations whom they exploited or served no such direct bond as would exclude their own mediation. Three thousand years ago their language was reflected in the names of half the landmarks and roadsteads of the sea—later the Greeks attempted to explain these names by punning upon their sound in some Greek dialect and fitting to each some fantastic legend.

As the Asiatics ran thus westward before the summer gales, their path was barred at last by the eastern shore of Barbary.

It is curious to note how specially designed was this coast, and especially its

The Phœnicians

north - eastern promontories, for the first landing-place of Asiatics upon our shores. The recess which is marked upon the map with an **X** and which is now called the Gulf of Tunis was designed in every way

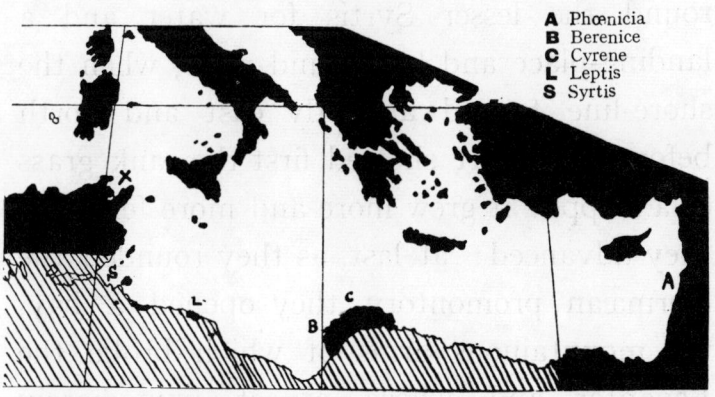

to arrest these merchants and to afford them opportunities for their future dominion.

They had sounded along the littoral of the desert: they were acquainted with the harbours which led them westward along the Libyan beach and with the little territories which were besieged all round by the sand and drew their life from the sea: where

The Bay of Carthage

later were to rise Cyrene and Berenice and Leptis.

They had seen the mirage all along that hot coast, and bare sandhills shimmering above shallow roadsteads: they had felt round the lesser Syrtis for water and a landing-place and had found none, when the shore-line turned abruptly east and north before them. It showed first the rank grass of a steppe; it grew more and more fertile as they advanced: at last, as they rounded the Hermæan promontory, they opened a bay, the mountainous arms of which broke the Levanter and whose aspect immediately invited them to beach their keels.

It stands at the narrow passage between the eastern and the western basins of the Mediterranean; and the western basin had not as yet been visited (it would seem) by men capable of developing its wealth. This bay upon which the Tyrians landed was sheltered and deep: there was, as in their

"Afrigya"

own country, a belt of fertile soil between the shore and the mountains; the largest river of Barbary was to hand. Their first settlements, of which Utica, near Porto Farina, was perhaps the earliest, began the new expansion of the Phœnician people. They called the shore their "Afrigya"—that is, their "colony." The word took root and remained. It was in this way that Asia, much older than we are, much more wily, not so brave, came in as a merchant and crept along till she found, and landed on, the Maghreb, where it stands out across the entry to the western seas.

When these first African cities had been founded for some centuries, there was built on the same gulf and at its head—perhaps as a depôt for Utica, more probably as a refuge for Tyrian exiles—a city called "The New Town": it is of this title, whose Semitic form must have resembled some such sound as "Karthadtha," that the Greeks made

Carchedon and the Latins Carthago, and it was from this centre that there arose and was maintained for seven hundred years over the Western Mediterranean an Oriental influence which was always paramount and threatened at certain moments to become universal and permanent.

Our race was not then conscious of itself. Gaul, Spain, the Alps and Italy north of the Apennines were a dust of tribes, villages and little fortified towns to which there was not to be given for many centuries the visible unity which we inherit from Rome. Rome itself was not yet walled. Southern Italy, though far more wealthy, was divided, and as for Africa it was full of roving men, Berbers, to whom some prehistoric chance, coupled with their soil and climate, had bequeathed such horses and such a tradition of riding as their descendants still possess. These savages must have felt in their blood that the Greek colonies, (when such towns were planted among them,)

Carthage

were of their own family and worshipped gods whom they could understand; just as, much later, they learnt to accept quite easily the kindred domination of the Italians: but the western instinct was still far too vague to permit of any coalition, or to react with any vigour against the newcomers from the east. It was not till travel, increasing wealth and the discipline of government had permitted the nomads to know themselves for Europeans that the presence of the foreigner became first irksome and then intolerable. It was not till nearly seven hundred years had passed that Rome, the centre and representative of the West, first conquered and then obliterated the power of Asia in this land.

Meanwhile Carthage grew pre-eminent, and as she grew, manifested to the full the spirit which had made her. Her citizens sailed through the Straits of Gibraltar; they knew the African and the Iberian coasts of the Atlantic. They may have

CARTHAGE

visited Britain. They crossed Gaul. It is said that they saw the Baltic. And everywhere they sought eagerly and obtained the two objects of their desire: metals and negotiation. In this quest, in spite of themselves, these merchants, who could see nothing glorious in either the plough or the sword, stumbled upon an empire. Their constitution and their religion are enough to explain the fate which befell it.

They were governed, as all such states have been, by the wealthiest of their citizens. It was an oligarchy which its enemies might have thought a mere plutocracy; its populace were admitted to such lethargic interference with public affairs as they might occasionally demand; perhaps they voted: certainly they did not rule; and the whole city enjoyed (as all such must enjoy) a peculiar calm. Civil war was unknown to it, for its vast mass of poorer members could not even be armed in the service of their country, save at a wage, and certainly had no military aptitudes to waste upon domestic quarrels. To such a people the furious valour of Roman and Greek disturbance must have seemed a vulgar anarchy, nor perhaps could they understand that the States which are destined alternately to dominate the world by thought or by armies are in every age those whose energy creates a perpetual conflict within themselves. It was characteristic of the Carthaginians that they depended for their existence upon a profound sense of security and that they based it upon a complete command of the sea. It was their contention that since no others could (to use their phrase) "wash their hands" in the sea without the leave of Carthage, their polity was immortal. They made no attempt to absorb or to win the vast populations from whom they claimed various degrees of allegiance. The whole Maghreb, and, later, Spain as well; the islands, notably the Balearics and Sardinia, were for them mere sources of wealth and of those mercenary troops which, in the moment of her fall, betrayed the town. When they contemplated their own greatness their satisfaction must have reposed upon the density of their population—their walls may have held more than half a million souls at a time when few towns of the west could count a tenth of such a number—upon their immemorial security from invasion, upon the excessive wealth of their great families (whose luxury the whole nation could contemplate with a vicarious satisfaction), upon the solidity of their credit, the resources of their treasury, and, above all, upon the excellent seamanship, the trained activity, and the overwhelming numbers of their navy.

As for their religion, it was of that dark inhuman sort which has in various forms tempted, and sometimes betrayed, ourselves. Gods remote and vengeful, an absence of those lesser deities and shrines which grace common experience and which attach themselves to local affections: perhaps some awful and unnamed divinity; certainly cruelty, silence and fear distinguished it. Even the goddess who presided over their loves had something in her at once obscene and murderous.

It is natural to those who are possessed by such servile phantasies that their worship should mix in with the whole of their lives and even penetrate to an immoderate degree those spheres of action which a happier and a saner philosophy is content to leave untrammelled. These dreadful deities of theirs afforded names for their leaders and served for a link between the scattered cities of their race: the common worship of Melcarth made an invisible bond for the whole Phœnician world; the greatest of the Carthaginian generals bore the title of " Baal's Grace."

With this gloomy and compelling faith and with this political arrangement there went such a social spirit as such things will breed. Not only were the Carthaginians content to be ruled by rich men always, but the very richest were even too proud for commerce; they lived as a gentry upon land and saw, beneath the merchants who were their immediate inferiors (and accustomed, it may be presumed, to purchase superior rank) a great herd of despicable and never laborious poor—incapable of rebellion or of foreign service. The very fields around the city were tilled, not by the Carthaginians, but by the half-breeds who had at least inherited something of western vigour and application.

When the crowd within the walls was too great, a colony would spring from its overflow into some distant harbour: emigrants led by one of those superiors without whom, as it seemed, the Phœnician was unable to act. It would appear that these daughter-nations were as averse to military sacrifice as their parent, and that they depended for their protection upon no effort of their own, but upon the fleet and the treasury of Carthage. In this way was built up a vast domain of colonies, tributaries and naval bases which was sporadic and ill organised in plan, enormous in extent, and of its nature lacking in permanence.

No system more corrupt or more manifestly doomed to extinction could be conceived, nor is it remarkable that when that system disappeared not a trace of it should remain among the millions whom it had attempted to command. Carthage had not desired to create, but only to enjoy: therefore she left us nothing. Her very alphabet was borrowed from our invention. Of seven hundred years during which the Asiatics had dominated Barbary nothing is left. The extinction of their power was indifferent or pleasing to the Mediterranean they had ruled; their language dwindled on through five hundred further years—its literature has been utterly forgotten. A doubtful derivation for the names of Cadiz, of Barcelona, and of Port Mahon, a certain one for Carthagena, are all that can be ascribed to-day to this fanatic and alien people: for they came of necessity into conflict with the Power that was to unify and direct the common forces of Europe.

At first the expansion of Carthage met with nothing more than could amuse its facile energies and increase its contemptuous security: it judged, exploited, or subsidised the barbaric tribes of Africa and Spain and Sardinia; it wrangled with the Greek colonies whom perhaps it thought itself "predestined" to rule—for to prophesy was a weakness in the blood from which it sprang. Some two centuries and a half before our era, when these Orientals had had footing for near a thousand and Carthage an existence

The Roman Attack

of six hundred years, Rome moved to the attack.

Rome had already achieved and was leading a confederation of the Italian peoples, she had already stamped her character and impressed her discipline upon the most advanced portion of the west, she had for a full generation minted that gold into coin, when she became aware that a city with whom she had often treated and whom she had thought remote, was present: something alien, far wealthier than herself, far more numerous and boasting a complete hold of communications and of the western sea. Between the two rivals so deep a gulf existed that the sentiment of honour in either was abhorrent or despicable to the other.

The Roman people were military. They had no love for ships. The sea terrified them: their expansion was by land and their horror of the sea explains much of their history. The very boast of maritime

The Punic Wars

supremacy that Carthage made was a sort of challenge to their genius. They accepted that challenge and their success was complete. Within a hundred years they had first tamed and then obliterated their rival, and the Maghreb re-entered Europe.

The first accidents of that conflict were of such a nature as to confirm Carthage in her creed and to lead her on to her destiny. She found, indeed, that the command of the sea was a doubtful thing: the landsmen beat her in the first round; clumsily and in spite of seamanship. But when, as a consequence of such defeat, they landed upon the African soil which she had thought inviolable, there, to her astonishment, she overwhelmed them. The loss of Sicily, to which she consented, did nothing to warn her. She became but the greater in her own eyes: Sicily she replaced by a thorough hold upon Spain, an expansion the more imperial that the new province was more distant and far larger,

The Punic Wars

and indefinitely more barbarous than the last. It may be imagined what a bitter patriotism the surprises of the early struggle had bred in the governing class of Carthage. From the moment when, in their unexpected victory, they had burnt the Roman soldiers alive to Moloch, this aristocracy had determined upon a final defeat of Rome. The greatest of them undertook the task and undertook it not from the Mother Country but from the Empire. He marched from Spain.

The Second Punic War is the best known of campaigns. Every Roman army that took the field was destroyed, the whole of Italy was open to the army of Hannibal, and (wherever that army was present—but only there) at his mercy. In spite of such miracles the Phœnician attempt completely failed. It failed for two reasons: the first was the contrast between the Phœnician ideal and our own; the second was the solidarity of the western blood.

The Failure

The army which Hannibal led recognised the voice of a Carthaginian genius, but it was not Carthaginian. It was not levied, it was paid. Even those elements in it which were native to Carthage or her colonies must receive a wage, must be "volunteer"; and meanwhile the policy which directed the whole from the centre in Africa was a trading policy. Rome "interfered with business"; on this account alone the costly and unusual effort of removing her was made.

The Europeans undertook their defence in a very different spirit: an abhorrence of this alien blood welded them together: the allied and subjugated cities which had hated Rome had hated her as a sister. The Italian confederation was true because it reposed on other than economic supports. The European passion for military glory survived every disaster, and above all that wholly European thing, the delight in meeting great odds, made our people strangely stronger for defeat.

OF CARTHAGE

The very Gauls in Hannibal's army, for all their barbaric anger against Rome, were suspected by their Carthaginian employers, and in Rome itself an exalted resolve, quite alien to the East and disconcerting to it, was the only result of misfortune.

Beyond the Mediterranean the Berber nomads, whose vague sense of cousinship with the Italians was chiefly shown in their contempt for the merchant cities, harassed Carthage perpetually; and when at last the Roman armies carried the war into Africa, Carthage fell. For somewhat more than fifty years she continued to live without security of territory or any honour, harassed by the nomad kings whom she dared not strike because they were the allies of Rome. She was still enormous in her wealth and numbers, it was only her honour that was gone; if indeed she had ever comprehended honour as did her rival.

The lapse of time brought no ease.

The Destruction

There was something in the temper of Asia that was intolerable to the western people. They saw it always ready to give way and then to turn and strike. They detested its jealous and unhappy rites. Its face was hateful and seemed dangerous to them. The two great struggles, at the close of which Rome destroyed as one destroys a viper, were conducted against members of the same family, Carthage and Jerusalem. A pretext was chosen: Carthage was abject, yielded three hundred hostages, and even all her arms. Only the matter of her religion moved her and the order to remove the site of the town. To this Carthage opposed a frenzy which delayed for three years the capture of the city; but when it was taken it was utterly destroyed. Every stone was removed, the land was left level, and suddenly, within a very few years of that catastrophe, every influence of Carthage disappeared. It was in this way that the first great power of the Orient upon the Maghreb was extinguished.

This final act of Rome was accomplished within a hundred and fifty years of the Nativity. The life of a man went by, and little more was done. It was close upon our era before the Roman habit took root in Africa, a century more before the Maghreb was held with any complete organisation. By the middle of the fifth century the Vandals had come in to ruin it.

There were, therefore, but little more than three hundred years during which Rome was to bring up this land into the general unity of Western Europe. There is no other portion of the world Rome governed, not even Southern Gaul, where her genius is more apparent. In that short interval of daylight—a tenth of the known history of the Maghreb—Rome did more than had Carthage in seven hundred years and more than was Islam to do in seven hundred more.

The Roman Monuments

It is indeed the peculiar mark of Barbary, which makes it a scene of travel different from all others, that everywhere the huge monuments of Rome stand out in complete desertion. If civilisation had been continuous here as it has been in nearly every city of Europe, Africa would not move one in this fashion. Or if a race, active and laborious, had quarried these stones to build new towns, their aspect would be more familiar, because in Europe we are accustomed to such decay and it helps us to

The Amphitheatre

forget the vast foundation of Rome. But to find it here, sometimes in the desert, nearly always in a solitude; to round a sandy hill without trees or men and to come, beyond a dry watercourse, upon these enormous evidences of our forerunners and their energy, is an impression Europe cannot give.

On the edge of the Sahara, in the very south of Tunis, where the salt of the waste is already upon one, there stands an arena of appalling size. It is smaller, but only a little smaller, than the Coliseum: it seems, in the silence and the glare, far larger. The Romans built it in their decline. You might as you watch it be in Rome or in Nîmes or in Arles, but you look around you and see the plain, and then the ruin grows fantastically broad and strong. Mountains are greatest when one wakes at morning and sees them unexpectedly after a long night journey; when the last sight one had by sunset was of low hills and meadows. So it is with

The Roman Planting

these ruins in Africa. The silence and the loneliness frame them. They are sudden, and when they have once been seen, especially by a man who wanders in that country on foot and does not know what marvel he may not find at the next turn of the path, they never afterwards leave the mind.

The things Rome did in Barbary were these : Of agriculture, which had been exceptional, despised by the cavalry of the mountains and confined to the little plains at the heads of the harbour-bays, she made a noble and, while she ruled, a permanent thing. Indeed it is one of the tests of the return of Europe to her own in the Maghreb that with the advance of our race, corn and vineyards advance, and with our retreat they recede. Rome planted trees which brought and stored rain. She most elaborately canalised and used the insufficient water of the high plateaux. She established a system of great roads. Where Carthage

OF TREES AND TOWNS

had produced the congestion of a few commercial centres, Rome spread out everywhere small flourishing and happy towns; a whole string of them along the coast in every bay from the Hippos to Tangier. There is, perhaps, not one of the little harbours backed up against the spurs of the Atlas, each in its bay, that has not a Roman market-place beneath its own. Here, as throughout the west, the civilisation of Rome was easy and desired, for it was in her temper to be of a conquering simplicity and in her chronicles she openly confessed her sins. The same unity which moulded Gaul was felt in Africa. The Roman arch and brick and column, the Roman road—all of one certain type—are as plain throughout the Maghreb as a thousand miles away in Treves or Rheims.

The desert was alien to Rome, as the sea was. The old trade from the Soudan which had been the staple of Leptis and which Carthage had certainly maintained,

The Legionaries

drooped and perhaps disappeared. Roman Africa turned to the Mediterranean and lived upon the commerce of its further shores. Along the edge of the Sahara a string of posts was held. Biskra was Roman, and El Kantara, and Gafsa. The doubt indeed is rather where the Romans did not penetrate, so tenacious were they in holding the southern boundary of Europe, the wall of the Atlas, against the wandering tribes of the sand. There is a fine story of a French commander who, having taken his column with great efforts through a defile where certainly men had never marched before, was proud, and sent a party to chisel the number of the regiment upon a smooth slab of rock above them, but when the men had reached it they saw in deep clear letters, cut long before, "The IIIrd Legion. The August. The Victorious."

Of twenty startling resurrections of Rome which a man sees in less than twenty days on

Verecunda

foot in any part of Algiers, consider this. Beyond Lamboesis, the frontier town of the Legionaries, with only a range of hills between it and the Sahara, there was a little town or village. It was quite small and a long way off from the city. It was of no importance; we have no record of it. Except that its name was Verecunda, we know nothing about it. One of its citizens, being grateful that he was born in his native place, thought he would give the little town or village a gate worthy of the love he bore it, and he built an arch all inspired with the weightiness of Rome.

The little town has gone. There is not a single stone of it left. But as you come round a grove of trees in a lonely part, under the height of Aures, you have before you this great thing, as though it were on the Campagna or carefully railed round in some very wealthy city.

It is all alone. The wind blows through it

The Great Arch

off the mountains. Every winter the frost opens some new little crack, and every generation or so a stone falls. But in two thousand years not so much has been ruined by time, but that the impression of Rome remains: its height, its absoluteness, and its strength. And this example is but one of very many that a man might choose as he wandered up and down the high steppes and through the gorges of the hills.

The Berbers

As he so wanders, he is taken with a strong desire to grasp the whole place at one view as it stood just before the barbarians came, and to see what the Vandals saw: to look up the valley from the rock of Cirta with the temples on the edge of either precipice and to see the towns re-arise. There are men who have felt this desire in Italy, but in Africa it is a much stronger desire, and since Africa is strange and very empty, perhaps by watching long enough at night that desire might be fulfilled.

Rome not only governed, but also made, Africa. The foundations on which the Maghreb is laid, and to which it must return, are Roman; the Berber race was no conscious part of us. I have said that it did not know itself until the Romans came, and when they came the Berbers slipped into the Roman unity more slowly and with more political friction, (but with less rebellion and therefore less proof of ill-ease,) than did the Gauls.

The Berbers

There is no more symbolic picture in the history of the Maghreb than the picture of Scipio clothing in the Roman dress that Massinissa, his ally, the king of the nomads who rode without stirrups or bridle.

The Berbers were not destined to preserve their Roman dignity. Something barbaric in them, something of the boundaries, of the marches, planted in these men (though they were, and still are, of our own kind) a genius for revolt. Let it be noted that in Africa every heresy arose. That Africa admitted the Vandals by treason, and that even when Africa accepted Islam, sect upon sect divided its history. Africa has always stood to the rest of the Empire as a sort of ne'er-do-weel: a younger son perpetually asking for adventure and rejecting discipline. To this the Roman horror of the sea lent a peculiar aid. Like Britain, Africa was cut off from the mainland. Like Britain, Africa was destined in the disruption of the Empire to lose the

The Arabs

Roman idiom and the traditions of orderly life; but with this difference, that Britain was reconquered by the religion and the manner of Europe within three generations of its loss: Africa was finally invaded, not by dull barbarians staring at the City and humble before her name, but by a brilliant cavalcade which galloped, driven forward by high convictions. The Arabs came in the seventh century, like a sort of youth contemptuous of the declining head of Rome. Barbary, then, I repeat, was swept into the Arabian language and religion in one cavalry charge, and that language and religion not only became immediately the masters of its people, but had twelve hundred years in which to take root and make a soil.

For about five hundred years, from a little after the birth of Our Lord to the close of the sixth century, our culture had been universal among the Berbers. In the last three centuries the Faith was dominant.

The Arabs

But rebellion was in them, and when the Arabs came the whole edifice suddenly crumbled.

Asia, which had first sailed in by sea and had been destroyed, or rather obliterated, when Carthage fell, came in now from the desert; Asia was like an enemy who is driven out of one vantage, and then, after a breathing-space, makes entry by another. But in such a struggle the periods of success and failure are longer than those of sieges, and even than the lives of kingdoms. The Maghreb, our test of sovereignty, had admitted the Phœnician for some six or seven hundred years. It had been thoroughly welded into Rome for five hundred. The Vandals came, and did no more than any other wandering tribe: they stirred the final anarchy a little; they were at once absorbed. But the tenacity by which Gaul, Britain, Spain and the Rhine were to slough off the memories of decay and to attain their own

The Arabs

civilisation again after the repose of the Dark Ages—that tenacity was not in the nature of Barbary.

In the seventh and eighth centuries, when all the remainder of the west had fallen, when Italy was already taxed and half governed by a few Germans, when Gaul and Spain had at their heads small bands of mixed barbarian and Roman nobles, and when everything seemed gone to ruin, this southern shore of the Mediterranean was overwhelmed and, what is more, persuaded.

There came riding upon it out of the desert continual lines of horsemen whom these horsemen of Numidia could mix with and understand. The newcomers wore the white wrapping of the south : all their ways were southern ways, suited to the intensity of the sun, and Barbary, or the main part of it, was southern and burning. Their eyes were very bright, and in their ornaments the half-

The Arabs

tamed tribesmen recognised an old appetite for splendour. For all the effect of Rome perhaps one-third of the African provincials were still nomadic when the Arabs appeared, and that nomadic part was thickest towards the desert from which the invasion came; the invaders themselves were nomads, and even on the shore of the Maghreb, where men had abandoned the nomadic habit, the instinct of roving still lingered.

Islam, therefore, when it first came in, tore up what Rome had planted as one tears up a European shrub planted in the friable soil of Africa.

The Bedawin, as they rode, bore with them also a violent and simple creed. And here, again, a metaphor drawn from the rare vegetation of this province can alone define the character of their arrival. Their Faith was like some plant out of the solitudes; it was hard in surface; it was simple in form; it was fitted rather to endure than to grow. It was

The Arabs

consonant with the waterless horizons and the blinding rocks from which it had sprung. Its victory was immediate. Before Charlemagne was born the whole fabric of our effort in Barbary, the traditions of St. Augustine and of Scipio, had utterly disappeared. No one from that time onwards could build a Roman arch of stone or drive a straight road from city to city or recite so much as the permanent axioms of the Roman Law.

Elsewhere, in Syria and in Asia and in Spain, the Mohammedans failed to extirpate Christianity, and were able for some centuries to enjoy the craftsmanship and the sense of order which their European subjects could lend them. It was only here, in Africa, that their victory was complete. Therefore it is only here, in Africa, that you see what such a victory meant, and how, when it was final, all power of creation disappeared. The works which have rendered

The Arabs

Islam a sort of lure for Europe were works that could not have been achieved save by European hands.

The Roman towns did not decay; they were immediately abandoned. Gradually the wells filled; the forests were felled in bulk; none were replanted. Of the Olive Gardens, the stone presses alone remain. One may find them still beneath the sand, recalling the fat of oil. But there, to-day, not a spear of grass will grow, and the Sahara has already crept in. The olives long ago were cut down for waste, or for building or for burning. There was not in any other province of the empire so complete an oblivion, nor is there any better example of all that "scientific" history denies: for it is an example of the cataclysmic—of the complete and rapid changes by which history alone is explicable: of the folly of accepting language as a test of origin: of the might and rapidity of religion (which is

The Atlas

like a fire): of its mastery over race (which is like the mastery of fire over the vessels it fuses or anneals): of the hierarchic nature of conquest: of the easy destruction of more complex by simpler forms. . . .

If one is to understand this surprising history of Barbary, and to know both what the Romans did in it and what the Arabs did, and to grasp what the reconquest has done or is attempting to do, it is necessary to examine the physical nature of this land.

Along all its hundreds of miles, the Maghreb is determined by Mount Atlas, or rather, the Maghreb is Atlas itself standing huge between the Sahara and the sea. It is a bulk of mountains so formed that one may compare it to a city wall with a broad top for fighting men to move on and a parapet along both the inner and the outer edges. The outer parapet, which is called " The

The Relief

Little Atlas," runs along the Mediterranean shore: the inner parapet, which is called "The Great Atlas," runs along the desert, and is usually the higher of the two chains. These two chains do not run quite parallel, but converge towards Tunis and spread apart towards the Atlantic; the table-land between them, which is called "The High Plateaux," and is in some places three thousand feet above the sea, broadens therefore from less than a hundred to well over two hundred miles across; but at either end it somewhat changes its character, for at the Tunis end it is too narrow to be a true plateau and becomes a jumble of mountains where the Greater and the Lesser Atlas meet, while in Morocco it becomes too broad to maintain its character and is diversified by continual subsidiary ranges. But in between these two extremities it is a true table-land with isolated summits rising here and there from it, and at their feet shallow and brackish lakes called *Shotts*, round which are rims of marshy reeds and, in summer, gleaming sheets of salt. For there is no drainage away from the table-land to the desert or to the sea, save where, here and there, a torrent (such as the Chélif or the Rummel) digs itself an erratic gorge and escapes through the coast range to the Mediterranean. These exceptions are very rare and they do not disturb the general plan of the country, which is everywhere constructed of the Atlas running in two ranges that hold up between them the plateau with its salt lakes and isolated groups of hills.

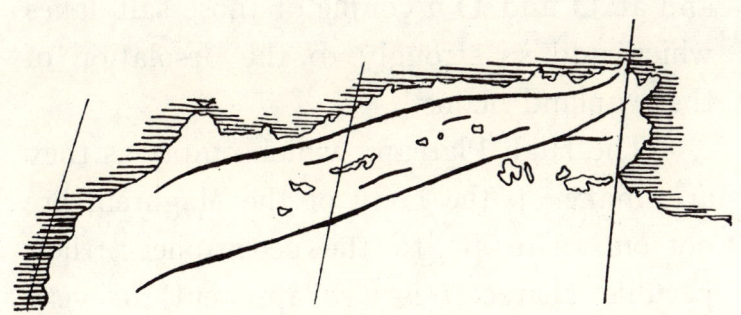

The Table-land

If, therefore, one were to take a section anywhere from north to south, from the Mediterranean to the Sahara, one would get some such figure as this:

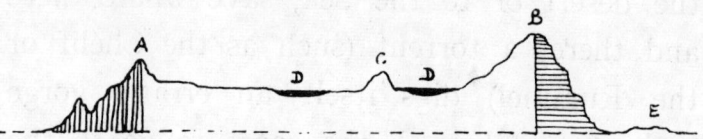

where the perpendicular shading on the left is the Mediterranean slope and drainage, the horizontal shading on the right, the desert slope, and where the Little Atlas is marked **A**, the Great Atlas **B** (falling down to **E**, the dunes of the Sahara), where at **C** is one of the isolated hills of the table-land, and at **D** and **D** a couple of those salt lakes which add so strongly to the desolation of these upland plains.

The High Plateaux, which, empty as they are, make up the body of the Maghreb, are not only a reality to the geographer: their peculiar character is also apparent to every

The Table-land

traveller who crosses them. The rise up to them from the Mediterranean, though confused, is observable; the fall from them to the Sahara is violent, and, through its central part, dramatic. It is not unusual for a man who has traversed this table-land upon more than one voyage to recall clefts in the southern and the northern ranges so placed that they were like windows through which one could look down upon the lower world.

These clefts resemble each other strangely. From steps of cliffs, rarely the one a man sees the limestone, the desert touched rarely and more by the green of palm-trees

The Table-land

and ending southward, glaring and arid and sharp, against the extremity of the horizon. From the other, he sees the woods of the coast, dense and well watered, mixing with the rocks about him, and right beyond the valley the pleasant line of the sea. But each of the views he carries in his mind has this in common, that he has seen it from a height, and looked down suddenly from a mountain table-land upon a flat below: to the north upon a level of waves over which went the shadows of clouds: to the south upon a level of sand stretching under a small and awful sun.

If a man were to live in this land, the High Plateaux would fill up the most of his mind, as they take up by far the most of the country itself in space. One is compelled to move when one is upon them. There is no resting-place: only, along the far edge, before the fall into the desert begins, the ruins of the Roman frontier towns. These

The Table-land

wastes hold the soul of Numidia. The horses of Barbary are native to them. It is said that these horses sicken on the seaboard—certainly their race dies on the northern shores of the Mediterranean unless it is crossed with one of our coarser breeds—for they were born to breathe this dry air and to make rapid prints with their unshod hoofs upon the powder of the plains and the salt.

The table-land, then, is the heart of the Maghreb, yet it has no name, not even among the wandering Arabs.

These come up on to it in spring from the hot desert below, driving slow files of proud and foolish camels. They pasture flocks in among the brushwood and by the rare streams; then when the autumn descends and the first cold appals them, before the winter scurries across these flats, they turn back and patiently go down the mountain roads into the Sahara, leaving the Berbers to them-

The Tell

selves again. For four months the plains above are swept with snow, and a traveller in that season, feeling the sharp and frozen dust in his face before the gale, and seeing far off bare cones of standing hills above salt marshes, thinks himself rather in Idaho or Nevada than here in Africa which Europe thinks so warm.

That belt of coast upon which Atlas descends is of a nature quite distinct from the High Plateaux. The Americans can match such sudden contrasts: we in Europe have nothing of the kind. You come down from salt water to fresh, from a cold (or from a burning) to a genial air, and you enter as you sink from the table-land a territory of great luxuriance. It is called the Tell, and to seize its character it is necessary to modify and to develop somewhat one's idea of the mountain chains. For though the Greater and the Lesser Atlas run in those main lines which appear in the little sketch upon page 58,

The Mountains

yet in detail each range, and especially the range along the sea, is broken and complex, and is made up of a number of separate folds, sometimes parallel and sometimes overlapping, thus:

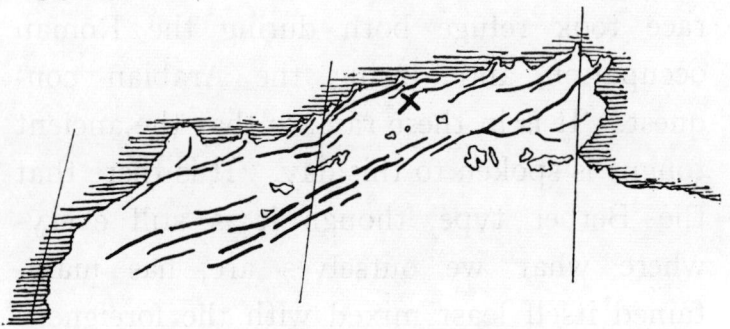

Moreover, the heights are irregular. There are groups of high peaks and ridges against the desert to the east in the Aurès Mountains, and to the west in those of Morocco, while along the seaboard great bulges of mountain rise in places from the Lower Atlas to a height rivalling the inland range. For instance, where an **X** is marked upon the sketch map, there is an almost isolated mass known as the Djurjura, very high, almost

The Berber Strongholds

as high as Aurès, which stands up 150 miles behind it above the Sahara. It was in these groups of higher and more rugged hills along the seaboard or the desert that the native languages and perhaps the purity of the native race took refuge both during the Roman occupation and during the Arabian conquest. It is in these ravines that the ancient tongue is spoken to this day. It is there that the Berber type, though it is still everywhere what we ourselves are, has maintained itself least mixed with the foreigner: it is even, perhaps, allied in these hills with a people older than we or the Berber can be.

The fact that the Lesser Atlas thus faces close upon the sea and falls upon it abruptly, determines an abundant rain-fall upon the Tell, and makes it fruitful. The fact that the Lesser Atlas consists of folds overlapping each other and running from north-east to south-west has furnished a multitude of bays, each lying between two spurs of the hills. Every

The Bays of the Tell

such bay has a harbour more or less important, and that harbour is nearly always upon the westerly side; for the prevalent strong wind, which is from the east, drives a current with it, and this current scours out the bays, clearing up and deepening the westerly shore, but leaving the eastern shallow. Thus Bone, Philippeville, Algiers, Calle, and Utica itself, which was the oldest of all, are on the westerly sides of such bays. Into each bay a mountain torrent falls, or sometimes a larger stream, and the long process of erosion has scoured all the coast into a network of valleys, so that, unless one has a clear view of the scheme in one's mind, one is bewildered and does not always know at what point in the upward journey one passes from the Tell to the High Plateaux, distinct as these regions are.

Thus a simple plan of a portion of the Tell is as given on the following page, where the line of crosses indicates the watershed

The Physical Constitution

between the Mediterranean and the inland drainage of the High Plateaux.

But if one were to mark on this map a stippled surface for contours under five hundred feet, a hatched one for the same between five and fifteen hundred, a black one up to

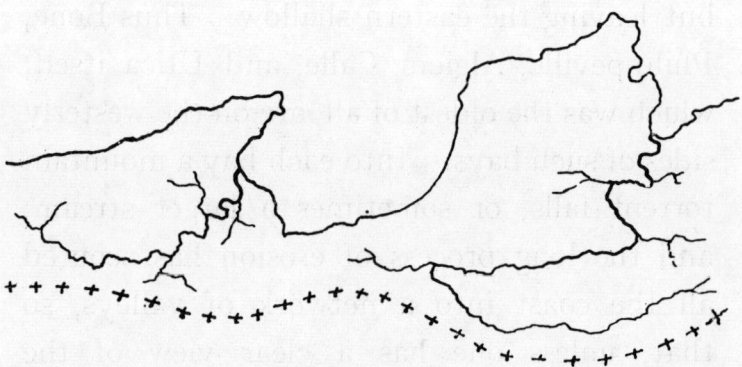

two thousand five hundred, and above that leave the heights in white with little triangles for the summits, one would get some such complicated scheme as is shown on the opposite page, where it will be seen that a high mountain (at **C**) overlooks the shore far from the watershed, and the scheme of valleys is complex and might seem a labyrinth to a man on foot without a map. At **A** and **B** are the ports of each bay, and near to each at the mouth of either river a large plain such as is characteristic of the heads of all these inlets. Their earth is black, deep, and fertile : inviting the plough. Such fields fed

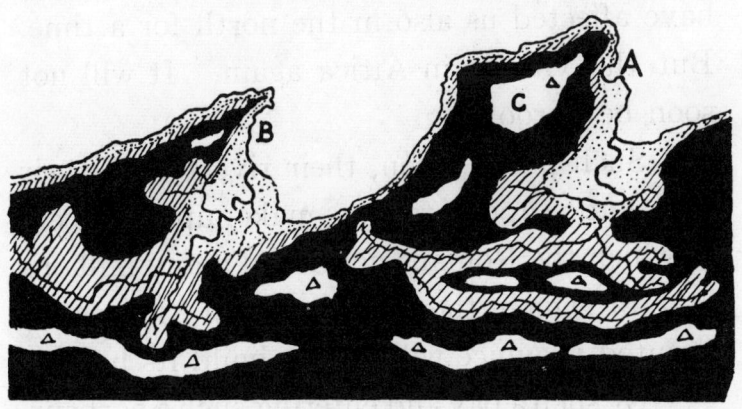

Utica, Icosium and Hippo Regius and Cæsarea. They remained wild and abandoned for over a thousand years, but to-day you may see miles of vineyards planted in rows that run converging to the limits of the plain, where, until this last generation, no one had dug or pruned or gathered or pressed

The New Vineyard

since the Latin language was forgotten in these lands. Indeed, it would be possible for a fantastic man to see in this replanting of the vine a symbol of the joy of Europe returning; for everywhere the people of the desert have had a fear of wine, and their powerful legends have affected us also in the north for a time. But the vine is in Africa again. It will not soon be uprooted.

Such plains, then, their rivers and their adjacent seaport towns, make up the Tell, in which the Romans nourished many millions and in which the most part of the reconstituted province will at last build its homes.

By such a bay and entering such a harbour, whoever comes to Africa reaches land.

* * * * *

It is perhaps at Bone, which stands to half a mile where Hippo stood, that the best introduction to Africa is offered. Here a mountain of conspicuous height rules an open roadstead full of shipping small and

The Bay of Hippo

large, and fenced round with houses for very many miles. A far promontory on the eastern side faces the western mountain, and half protects the harbour from summer gales. Below the mountain, the plain belonging to this bay stretches in a large half-circle,

marked only here and there with buildings but planted everywhere with olives, vines and corn. In the midst of this great flat stands up a little isolated hill, a sort of acropolis, and from its summit, from a window of his monastery there, St. Augustine, looking at that sea, wrote *Ubi magnitudo, ibi veritas*.

Hippo

The town is utterly gone. There are those who argue that this or that was not done as history relates, because of this or that no vestige remains; and if tradition tells them that Rome built here or there, they deny it, because they cannot find walls, however much they dig (within the funds their patrons allow them). These men are common in the universities of Europe. They are paid to be common. They should see Hippo.

Here was a great town of the Empire. It detained the host of Vandals, slaves and nomads for a year. It was the seat of the most famous bishopric of its day, and within its walls, while the siege still endured, St. Augustine died. It counted more than Palermo or Genoa: almost as much as Narbonne. It has completely disappeared. There are not a few bricks scattered, nor a line of Roman tiles built into a wall. There is nothing. A farmer in his ploughing once

Calama

disturbed a few fragments of mosaic, but that is all : they can make a better show at Bignor in the Sussex weald, where an unlucky company officer shivered out his time of service with perhaps a hundred men.

In the heart of the Tell, behind the mountains which hide the sea, yet right in the storms of the sea, in its clouds and weather, stands a little town which was called Calama in the Roman time and is now, since the Arabs, called Guelma.

It is the centre of that belt of hills. A broad valley, one of the hundreds which build up the complicated pattern of the Mediterranean slope, lies before the platform upon which the fortress rose. A muddy river nourishes it, and all the plain is covered with the new farms and vineyards—beyond them the summits and the shoulders that make a tumbled landscape everywhere along the northern shores of Africa guard the place whichever way one turns.

Calama

From the end of every street one sees a mountain.

If a man had but one day in which to judge the nature of the province, he could not do better than come to this town upon some winter evening when it was already dark, and wake next morning to see the hurrying sky and large grey hills lifting up into that sky all around and catching the riot of its clouds. It is high and cold: there is a spread of pasture in its fields and a sense of Europe in the air. No device in the architecture indicates an excessive heat in summer and even the trees are those of Italy or of Provence. Its site is a survival from the good time when the Empire packed this soil with the cities of which so great a number have disappeared: it is also a promise of what the near future may produce, a new harvest of settled and wealthy walls, for it is in the refounding of such municipalities that the tradition of Europe will work upon Africa

Calama

and not in barren adventure southward towards a sky which is unendurable to our race and under which we can never build and can hardly govern.

Guelma is typical in every way. It was Berber before the Romans came, but nothing remains of its founders or of whatever punic influence its first centuries may have felt. Of Rome so much endures that the heavy walls and the arches are, as it were, the framework of the place.

In the citadel a great fragment larger than anything else in the town runs right across the soldiers' quarters, pierced with the solid arches that once supported the palace.

The Permanence

of Calama. Only the woodwork has disappeared. The stones which supported the flooring still stand out unbroken, and the whole wall, though it is not very high—hardly higher than the big barracks around it—remains in the mind, as though it had a right to occupy one's memory of the Kasbah by a sort of majesty which nothing that has been built since its time has inherited. Here, as throughout the Empire, the impression of Rome is as indefinable as it is profound, but one can connect some part of it at least with the magnitude of the stones and the ponderous simplicity of their courses, with the strength that the half-circle and the straight line convey, and with the double evidence of extreme antiquity and extreme endurance; for there is something awful in the sight of so many centuries visibly stamped upon the stone, and able to evoke every effect of age but not to compel decay.

This nameless character which is the

mark of the Empire, and carries, as it were, a hint of resurrection in it, is as strong in what has fallen as in what stands. A few bricks built at random into a mud wall bear the sign of Rome and proclaim her title : a little bronze unearthed at random in the rubbish heaps of the Rummel is a Roman Victory : a few flag-stones lying broken upon a deserted path in the woodlands is a Roman Road : nor do any of these fragments suggest the passing of an irrecoverable good, but rather its continued victory. To see so many witnesses small and great is not to remember a past or a lost excellence, but to become part of it and to be conscious of Rome all about one to-day. It is a surety also for the future to see such things.

There is a field where this perpetuity and this escape from Time refresh the traveller with peculiar power. It is a field of grass in the uplands across which the wind blows with vigour towards distant hills. Here a peasant

The Peasant's Wall

of the place (no one knows when, but long ago) fenced in his land with Roman stones. The decay of Islam had left him aimless, like all his peers. He could not build or design. He could not cut stone or mould brick. When he was compelled to enclose his pasture, the only material he could use was the work of

the old masters who had trained his fathers but whom he had utterly forgotten or remembered only in the vague name of "Roum." It was long before the reconquest that he laboriously raised that wall. Some shadow of Turkish power still ruled him from Constantine. No one yet had crossed the sea from Europe to

The Landscape of Antiquity

make good mortar or to saw in the quarries again. It is with a lively appreciation that one notes how all he did is perishing or has perished. The poor binding he put in has crumbled. The slabs slope here and there. But the edges of those stones, which are twenty times older than his effort, remain. They will fall again and lie where he found them; but they and the power that cut them are alike imperishable.

It has been said that the men of antiquity had no regard for landscape, and that those principal poems upon which all letters repose betray an indifference to horizons and to distant views. The objection is ill-found, for even the poems let show through their admirable restraint the same passion which we feel for hills, and especially for the hills of home: they speak also of land-falls and of returning exiles, and an Homeric man desired, as he journeyed, to see far-off the smoke rising from his own fields and after that to die. But much stronger than anything their careful verse can give us of this appetite for locality is the emplacement of their buildings.

Mr. March-Phillips has very well described the spirit which built a certain temple into the scenery of a Sicilian valley. Here (he says), in a place now deserted, the white pillars ornament a jutting tongue of land, and are so placed that all the lines of the gorge lead up to them, and that the shrine becomes the centre of a picture, and, as it were, of a composition. Of this antique consciousness of terrestrial beauty all southern Europe is full, and here in Guelma, upon an edge of the high town, the site of the theatre gives evidence of the same zeal.

The side of a hill was chosen, just where the platform of the city breaks down sharply upon the plain below. There, so that the people and the slaves upon the steps could have a worthy background for their plays, the half-circle of the auditorium was cut out

The Theatre of Calama

like a quarry from the ground. Beyond the actors, and giving a solemnity to the half-religious concourse of the spectators, the mountains of the Tell stood always up behind the scene, and the height, not only of those summits but of the steps above the plain, enhanced the words that were presented. We have to-day in Europe no such aids to the senses. We have no such alliance of the air and the clouds with our drama, nor even with our patriotism—such as the modern world has made it.

The last centuries of the Empire had all these things in common: great verse inherited from an older time, good statuary, plentiful fountains, one religion, and the open sky. Therefore its memory has outlasted

THE GREATNESS OF

all intervening time, and it itself the Empire, (though this truth is as yet but half-received,) has re-arisen.

* * * * *

There is one great note in the story of our race which the least learned man can at once appreciate, if he travels with keen eyes looking everywhere for antiquity, but which the most learned in their books perpetually ignore, and ignore more and more densely as research develops. That note is the magnitude of the first four centuries.

Everybody knows that the ancient world ran down into the completed Roman Empire as into a reservoir, and everybody knows that the modern world has flowed outwards from that reservoir by various channels. Everybody knows that this formation of a United Europe was hardly completed in the first century, that it was at last conscious of disintegration in the fifth. The first four centuries are therefore present as dates in

The First Four Centuries

everybody's mind, yet the significance of the dates is forgotten.

Historians have fallen into a barren contemplation of the Roman decline, and their readers with difficulty escape that attitude. Save in some few novels, no writer has attempted to stand in the shoes of the time and to see it as must have seen it the barber of Marcus Aurelius or the stud-groom of Sidonius' Palace. We know what was coming, the men of the time knew it no more than we can know the future. We take at its own self-estimate that violent self-criticism which accompanies vitality, and we are content to see in these 400 years a process of mere decay.

The picture thus impressed upon us is certainly false. There is hardly a town whose physical history we can trace, that did not expand, especially towards the close of that time. There was hardly an industry or a class (notably the officials) that had not by an accumulation of experience grown to create upon a larger and a larger scale its peculiar contribution to the State ; and far the larger part of the stuff of our own lives was created, or was preserved, by that period of unity.

That our European rivers are embanked and canalised, that we alone have roads, that we alone build well and permanently, that we alone in our art can almost attain reality, that we alone can judge all that we do by ideas, and that therefore we alone are not afraid of change and can develop from within—in a word, that we alone are Christians we derive from that time.

Our theory of political justice was partly formulated, partly handed on, by those generations ; our whole scheme of law, our conceptions of human dignity and of right. Even in the details our structure of society descends from that source : we govern, or attempt to govern, by representation because the monastic institutions of the end of the Empire were under a necessity of

The First Four Centuries

adopting that device : we associate the horse with arms and with nobility because the last of the Romans did so.

If a man will stand back in the time of the Antonines and will look around him and forward toward our own day, the consequence of the first four centuries will at once appear. He will see the unceasing expansion of the paved imperial ways. He will conceive those great Councils of the Church which would meet indifferently in centres 1500 miles apart, in the extremity of Spain or on the Bosphorus : a sort of moving city whose vast travel was not even noticed nor called a feat. He will be appalled by the vigour of the western mind between Augustus and Julian when he finds that it could comprehend and influence and treat as one vast State what is even now, after so many centuries of painful reconstruction, a mosaic of separate provinces. He will calculate with what rapidity and uniformity the orders of those emperors who seem to us the lessening despots of a failing state were given upon the banks of the Euphrates, to be obeyed upon the Clyde. He will then appreciate why the Rome which Europe remembers, and upon which it is still founded, was not the Rome of literature with its tiny forum and its narrow village streets, but something gigantic like that vision which Du Bellay had of a figure with one foot upon the sunrise and its hands overspreading ocean.

Indeed this great poet expresses the thing more vividly by the sound of three lines of his than even the most vivid history could do.

> " Telle que dans son char la Bérycynthienne
> Couronnée de tours, et heureuse d'avoir
> Enfanté tant de dieux . . ."

This was the might and the permanence from which we sprang.

To establish the character of the Empire and its creative mission is the less easy from

The First Four Centuries

the prejudice that has so long existed against the action of religion, and especially of that religion which the Empire embraced as its cataclysm approached. The acceptation of the creed is associated in every mind with the eclipse of knowledge and with a contempt for the delights which every mind now seeks. It is often thought the cause, always the companion, of decay, and so far has this sentiment proceeded that in reading books upon Augustine or upon Athanasius one might forget by what a sea and under what a sunlight the vast revolution was effected.

It is true that when every European element had mixed to form one pattern, things local and well done disappeared. The vague overwhelming and perhaps insoluble problems which concern not a city but the whole world, the discovery of human doom and of the nature and destiny of the soul, these occupied such minds as would in an earlier time have bent themselves to simpler and more feasible tasks than the search after finality. It is true that plastic art, and to a less extent letters, failed: for these fringes of life whose perfection depends upon detail demand for their occasional flowering small and happy States full of fixed dogmas and of certain usages. But though it lost the visible powers antiquity had known, the Empire at its end, when it turned to the contemplation of eternity, broadened much more than our moderns—who are enemies of its religious theory—will admit. The business which Rome undertook in her decline was so noble and upon so great a scale that when it had succeeded, then, in spite of other invasions, the continuity of Europe was saved. We absorbed the few barbarians of the fifth century, we had even the vitality to hold out in the terror and darkness of the ninth, and in the twelfth we re-arose. It was the character of the Western Empire during the first four centuries, and notably its character towards

The First Four Centuries

their close, which prevented the sleep of the Dark Ages from being a death. These first four centuries cast the mould which still constrains us; they formed our final creed, they fixed the routes of commerce and the sites of cities, and perpetually in the smallest trifles of topography you come across them still: the boundary of Normandy, as we know it to-day, was fixed by Diocletian. If there can be said of Europe what cannot be said of any other part of the world, that its civilisation never grew sterile and never disappeared, then we owe the power of saying such a thing to that long evening of the Mediterranean.

* * * * *

If this pre-eminence of Rome in the process of her conversion is the lesson of all travel it is especially the lesson of Africa; and nowhere is that lesson taught more clear than in Guelma. Here also you may perceive how it was that the particular cause

The Arabic Influence

which ruined the spirit of the Roman town also saved its stones, and you may feel, like an atmosphere, the lightness, the permeation, as it were, without pressure:—the perpetual fluid influence which overflowed the province upon the arrival of the Arabs. So that the bone of Rome remain, caught in a drift of ideas which, like fine desert sand, could preserve them for ever.

For the Arab did in Calama what he did throughout Barbary: he cast a spell. He did not destroy with savagery, he rather neglected all that he could afford to neglect. Here also he cut down timber, but he did not replant. Here also he let the water-pipes of the Romans run dry. Here also the Arab, who apparently achieved nothing material, imposed a command more powerful than the compulsion of any government or the fear of any conqueror: he sowed broadcast his religion and his language; his harvest grew at once; first it hid and at last it stifled the religion

The Arabic Influence

and the language he had found. The speech, and the faith which renders that speech sacred, transformed the soul of Barbary: they oppose between them a barrier to the reconquest more formidable by far than were the steppes and the nomads to the first advance of Rome. Of this impalpable veil which is spread between the native population and the new settlers the traveller is more readily aware in the little cities of the hills than in the larger towns of the coast. The external change of the last generation is apparent: the houses about him are European houses; the roads might be roads in France or Northern Italy. The general aspect of Guelma confirms that impression of modernity, nor is there much save the low loop-holed walls which surround the town, to remind one of Africa; but from the midst of its roofs rises the evidence of that religion which still holds and will continue to hold all its people. The only building upon which the efforts of an

The Arabic Influence

indolent creed have fastened is the mosque, and the minaret stands alone, conspicuous and central over all the European attempt, and mocks us.

Far off, where the walls and the barracks are confused into a general band of white, and no outline is salient enough to distinguish the modern from the ancient work of the place, this wholly Mohammedan shaft of stone marks the place for Mohammedan. It is an enduring challenge.

There is a triumph of influence which all of us have known and against which many of us have struggled. It is certainly not a force which one can resist, still less is it effected by (though it often accompanies) the success of armies.

The Arabic Influence

It is the pressure and at last the conquest of ideas when they have this three-fold power: first, that they are novel and attack those parts of the mind still sensitive; secondly, that they are expounded with conviction (conviction necessary to the conveyance of doctrine); and, thirdly, that they form a system and are final. Such was the triumph of the Arab.

Our jaded day, which must for ever be taking some drug or tickling itself with unaccustomed emotion, has pretended to discover in Islam, as it has pretended to discover in twenty other alien things, the plan of happiness ; and a stupid northern admiration for whatever has excited the wonder or the curiosity of the traveller has made Mohammedism, as it has made Buddhism and God knows what other inferiorities or aberrations of human philosophy, the talk of drawing-rooms and the satisfaction of lethargic men. It is not in this spirit that a worthy tribute

The Arabic Invasion

can be paid to the enormous invasion of the seventh century.

That invasion as a whole has failed. Christendom, for ever criticised, (for it is in its own nature to criticise itself,) has emerged; but if one would comprehend how sharp was the issue, one should read again all that was written between Charlemagne and the death of St. Louis. In the Song of Roland, in the "Gesta Francorum," in Joinville, this new attack of Asia is present—formidable, and greater than ourselves; something which we hardly dared to conquer, which we thought we could not conquer, which the greatest of us thought he had failed in conquering. Islam was far more learned than we were, it was better equipped in arms and nevertheless more civic and more tolerant. When the last efforts of the crusades dragged back to Europe an evil memory of defeat, there was perhaps no doubt in those who despaired, still less in those who secretly delighted that such fantasies were

Its Continued Influence

ended—there was no doubt, I say, in their minds that the full re-establishment of our civilisation was impossible, and that the two rivals were destined to stand for ever one against the other: the invader checked and the invaded prudent; for, throughout the struggle we had always looked upon our rivals at least as equals and usually as superiors.

It is in the most subtle expressions that the quarrel between the two philosophies appears. Continually Islam presses upon us without our knowing it. It made the Albigenses, it is raising here and there throughout European literature at this moment notes of determinism, just as that other influence from the Further East is raising notes of cruelty or of despair.

There is one point in which the contact between these master-enemies and ourselves is best apparent. They gave us the Gothic, and yet under our hands the Gothic became the most essentially European of all European

The Gothic

things. Consider these two tiers of one Arabian building founded in Africa, while yet the vigour of that civilisation was strong. True, the work is not in stone but in plaster, for to work stone they needed an older civilisation than their own. But see how it is the origin of, or rather identical with, our ogive. By what is it that we recognise these intersecting segments (which are of the perfect 60° like our own) to be something foreign? And how is it that we know that no Christian could have built these things? Venice has windows like these: by just so much she is not of the West, and by just that innoculation

The Gothic

perhaps she perished. The ecstasy of height, the self-development of form into further form, the grotesque, the sublime and the enthusiastic—all these things the Arab arch lacks as utterly as did the Arab spirit; yet the form is theirs and we obtained it from them. In this similarity and in these differences are contained and presented visibly the whole story of our contact with them and of our antagonism.

In the presence of the doom or message which the Arabians communicated to our race in Africa, one is compelled to something of the awe with which one would regard a tomb from which great miracles proceeded, or a dead hero who, though dead, might not be disturbed. The thing we have to combat, or which we refrain and dread from combating, is not tangible, and is the more difficult to remove. It has sunk into the Atlas and into the desert, it has filled the mind of every man from the Soudan which it

The Touaregs

controls up northwards to Atlas and throughout this land.

Roaming in the Sahara are bands of men famous for their courage and their isolation. They are called the Touaregs. They are of the same race and the same language as those original Berbers who yet maintain themselves apart in the heights of Aurès or of the Djurdjura. They are the enemies of all outside their tribes, especially of the Arab merchants, upon whose caravans they live by pillage. Yet even these Islam has thoroughly possessed and would seem to have conquered for ever. Their language has escaped; their tiny literature (for they have letters of their own, and their alphabet is indigenous) has survived every external influence, but even there the God of the Mohammedans has appeared.

One taken captive some years since wrote back from Europe to his tribe in his own stiff characters a very charming letter in which he

The Touaregs

ended by recommending himself to the young women of his home, for he himself was a fighter, courteous, and in his thirtieth year. But when he had written " Salute the Little Queens from me," he was careful to add an invocation to Allah. And if in their long forays it is necessary to bury hastily some companion who has fallen in the retreat, his shallow grave in the sand is carefully designed according to the custom of religion. They leave him upon his right side in an attitude which they hold as sacred, his face turned to the east and towards Mecca. In this posture he awaits the Great Day.

Against this vast permanent and rooted influence we have nothing to offer. Our designs of material benefit or of positive enlightenment are to the presence of this common creed as is some human machine to the sea. We can pass through it, but we cannot occupy it. It spreads out before our advance, it closes up behind.

Nor will our work be accomplished until we have recovered, perhaps through disasters suffered in our European homes, the full tradition of our philosophy and a faith which shall permeate all our actions as completely as does this faith of theirs.

That no religion brought by us stands active against their own is an apparent weakness in the reconquest, but that consequence of the long indifference through which Europe has passed is not the only impediment it has produced. The dissolution of the principal bond between Europeans—the bond of their traditional ritual and confession—has also prevented the occupation of Africa from being, as it should have been, a united and therefore an orderly campaign of the West to recover its own.

Had not our religion suffered the violent schisms which are now so slowly healing, and had not our general life resolved itself for a time into a blind race between the various

An Opposing Faith

provinces of Europe, the reconquest of Barbary would have fallen naturally to the nations which regard each its own section of the opposing coast; as in the reconquest of Spain the Asturias advanced upon Leon, the Galicians upon Portugal, and Old Castille upon the southern province to which it extended its own name. Then Italy would have concerned itself with Tunis—with Ifrigya, that is—and with the rare fringe of the Tripolitan and its shallow harbours. The French would have occupied Numidia. The Spaniards would have swept on to re-Christianise the last province of the west from Oran to the Atlantic, and so have completed the task which they let drop after the march upon Granada. Such should have been the natural end of mediæval progress, and that reconstruction of the Empire (which was the nebulous but constant goal towards which the Middle Ages moved) would have been accomplished. But the most sudden and the most inexplicable of our revolutions came in and broke the scheme. The Middle Ages died without a warning. A curious passion for metaphysics seized upon certain districts of the north, which in their exaltation attempted to live alone : the south, in resisting the disruption of Europe, exhausted its energies ; and meanwhile the temptation to exploit the Americas and the Indies drained the Mediterranean of adventurers and of navies. Islam in its lethargy acquired new vigour from its latest converts, and the Turks, with none but the Venetians to oppose them, tore away from us the whole of the Levant and rode up the Danube to insult the centre of the continent. The European system flew apart, and its various units moved along separate paths with various careers of hesitation or of fever. It was not until the Revolution and the reconstitution of sane government among us that the common scheme of the west could reappear.

French Action

On this account—on account of the vast disturbance which accompanied the Reformation and the Renaissance—Europe halted for three centuries. When at last a force landed upon the southern shore of the Mediterranean, it was a force which happened to be despatched by the French.

The vices and the energy of this people are well known. They are perpetually critical of their own authorities, and perpetually lamenting the decline of their honour. There is no difficulty they will not urmount. They have crossed all deserts and have perfected every art. Their victories in the field would seem legendary were they not attested; their audacity, whether in civil war or in foreign adventure, has permanently astonished their neighbours to the south, the east and the north. They are the most general in framing a policy and the most actual in pursuing it. Their incredible achievements have always the appearance of accidents. They

The French

are tenacious of the memory of defeats rather than of victories. They change more rapidly and with less reverence than any other men the external expression of their tireless effort, yet, more than any other men, they preserve —in spite of themselves—an original and unchanging spirit. Their boundaries are continually the same. They are acute and vivid in matters of reason, careless in those of judgment. A coward and a statesman are equally rare among them, yet their achievements are the result of prudence and their history is marked by a succession of silent and calculating politicians. Alone of European peoples the Gauls have, by a sort of habit, indulged in huge raids which seemed but an expense of military passion to no purpose. They alone could have poured out in that tide of the third century before our era to swamp Lombardy, to wreck Delphi, and to colonise Asia. They alone could have conceived the crusades: they alone the

The French

revolutionary wars. It is remarkable that in all such eruptions they alone fought eastward, marching from camp into the early light; they alone were content to return with little spoil and with no addition of provinces, to write some epic of their wars.

It is evident that such a people would produce in Africa, not a European and a general, but a Gallic and a particular effect. They boast themselves in everything the continuators of the Romans. They do, indeed, inherit the Roman passion for equality, and they, like the Romans, have tenaciously fought their way to equality by an effort spread over many hundred years. They are Roman in their careful building, in their strict roads, in their small stature, in their heavy chests, in their clarity of language, in their adoration of office and of symbol, in their lightning marches: the heavy lading of their troops, their special pedantry, their disgust at vagueness, their ambition and their honour are

The French

Roman. But they are not Roman in permanent stability of detail. The Romans spread an odour of religion round the smallest functions of the State : of the French you can say no more than that any French thing you see to-day may be gone to-morrow, and that only France remains. They are not Roman in the determination never to retreat, nor are they Roman in the worship of silence. The French can express the majesty of the Empire in art : they cannot act it in their daily life—for this inheritance of Rome the Spaniards are better suited. As for the Roman conception of a fatal expansion the Russians exceed them, and for the Roman ease and aptitude the Italians.

Had, then, the reconquest of Barbary fallen naturally to the three sisters—to Spain, to Italy, and to France, the long attempt of Europe might have reached its end. The Spaniard would have crushed and dominated in Morocco where the Mohammedan was most

The French

strongly entrenched; the Italian, with his subtle admixture, would have kneaded Tunis and the eastern march into a firm barrier; the French would have developed their active commerce upon the many small towns of the Central Tell, would have pierced, as they are fitted to pierce, the high Central Plateaux with admirable roads, and would have garrisoned, as their taste for a risk well fits them to garrison, the outposts of the Central Atlas against the desert. Then the task would be over, and Europe would be resettled within its original boundaries.

* * * * *

On their long route marches, on the marches of their manœuvres and their wars, the French, along their roads which are direct and august, (and at evening, when one is weary, sombre,) seek a place of reunion and of repose: upon this the corps converges, and there at last a man may lie a long night under shelter and content to sleep: a town lies

The March

before the pioneers and is their goal. It stands, tiny with spires, above the horizon of their hedgeless plains, and as they go they sing of the halt, or, for long spaces, are silent, bent trudging under the pack: for they abhor parade. Very often they do not reach their goal. They then lie out in bivouac under the sky and light very many fires, five to a company or more, and sleep out unsatisfied. Such a strain and such an attempt: such a march, such a disappointment, and such a goal are the symbols of their history; for they are perpetually seeking, under arms, a Europe that shall endure. In this search they must continue here in Africa, as they continue in their own country, that march of theirs which sees the city ever before it and yet cannot come near to salute the guard at the gates and to enter in. It is their business to re-create the Empire in this province of Africa. It may be that here also they will come to no completion; but if they fail, Europe will fail

The French Genius

with them, and it will be a sign that our tradition has ended.

They have done the Latin thing. First they have designed, then organised, then built, then ploughed, and their wealth has come last. The mind is present to excess in the stamp they have laid upon Africa. Their utter regularity and the sense of will envelop the whole province; and their genius, inflexible and yet alert, alert and yet monotonous, is to be seen everywhere in similar roads, similar bridges of careful and even ornamented stone, similar barracks and loopholed walls.

There is a perspective upon the High Plateaux which though it is exceptional is typical of their spirit. It is on the salt plain just before the gate of the desert is reached and the fall on to the desert begun. Here the flat and unfruitful level glares white and red: it is of little use to men or none. Some few adventurers, like their peers in the Rockies, have

The Straight Railway

attempted to enclose a patch or two of ground, but the whole landscape is parched and dead. Through this, right on like a gesture of command, like the dart of a spear, goes the rail, urging to-

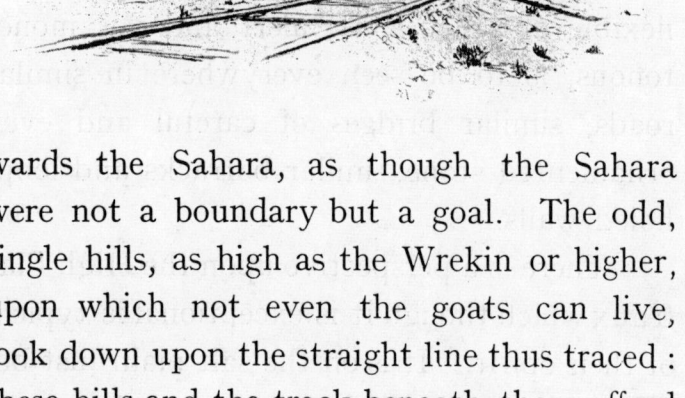

wards the Sahara, as though the Sahara were not a boundary but a goal. The odd, single hills, as high as the Wrekin or higher, upon which not even the goats can live, look down upon the straight line thus traced: these hills and the track beneath them afford a stupendous contrast. Nowhere is the determination of man more defiant against the sullen refusal of the earth.

There is another effort of the French

The French Afforestation

which may be watched with more anxiety and more comprehension by northern men than their admirable roads or their railways or their wires above the sand, and that is their afforestation.

It is a debate which will not be decided (for the material of full decision is lacking) whether, since the Romans crowded their millions into this Africa, the rainfall has or has not changed. It is certain that they husbanded water upon every side and built great barricades to hold the streams; yet it is certain, also, that their cities stood where no such great groups of men could live to-day. There are those who believe that under Atlas, towards the desert, a shallow sea spread westward from the Mediterranean and from Syrtis: there are others who believe that the dry water-courses of the Sahara were recently alive with streams, and that the tombs and inscriptions of the waste places, now half buried in the sand, prove a great lake upon

The French Afforestation

whose shores a whole province could cultivate and live. Both hypotheses are doubtful for this reason—that no good legend preserves the record. Changes far less momentous have left whole cycles of ballads and stories behind them. The Sahara has been the Sahara since men have sung or spoken of it. Moreover, the Romans did certainly push out, as the French have done, towards certain limits, beyond which no effort was worth the while of armies. They felt a boundary to the south. They could bear the summer of Biskra, but not that of Touggourt: their posts upon the edge of the desert were ultimate posts as are the European garrisons to-day.

But in one thing the sense of change is justified, and that is the fall of the woods. Here Islam worked itself out fully: its ignorance of consequence, its absolute and insufficient assertion, its lack of harmony with the process and modulation of time, its Arabian origin, are all apparent in the destruction of trees.

The French Afforestation

If the rainfall is as abundant as ever, it is not held, for the roots of trees are lacking, and if it be true that trees in summer bring rain of themselves by their leaves, then that benefit is also gone. There are many deep channels, called *secchias*, traversing the soft dust of the uplands, with no trace of bridges where the Roman roads cross them: they are new. They are carved by the sudden spates that follow the cloudbursts in the hills. Here, perhaps, in the Roman time were regular and even streams, and perhaps, upon their banks, where now are stretches of ugly earth quite bare, the legionaries saw meadows. At any rate, the trees have gone.

Up in the higher hills, in Aurés and the Djurjura, upon the flanks of the mountains where the Berbers remain unconquered, and where the melting of the snows give a copious moisture, forests still remain. They are commonly of great cedars as dark as the pine woods of the Vosges or the noble chesnut groves by

The French Afforestation

which the Alps lead a man down into Italy. But these forests are rare and isolated as the aboriginal languages and tribes which haunt them. You may camp under the deep boughs within a march of Batna and then go northward and eastward for days and days of walking before you come again to the woods and their scent and their good floor of needles in the heights from which you see again the welcome of the Mediterranean.

This lack of trees the French very labo-

Story of the Determinist

riously attempt to correct. Their chief obstacle is the nature of that religion which is also the hard barrier raised against every other European thing which may attempt to influence Africa to-day.

There was a new grove planted some ten years since in a chosen place. It was surrounded with a wall, and the little trees were chosen delicately and bought at a great price, and planted by men particularly skilled. Also, there was an edict posted up in those wilds (it was within fifty miles of the desert, just on the hither side of Atlas) saying that a grove had been planted in such and such a place and that no one was to hurt the trees, under dreadful penalties. The French also, as is the laudable custom of Republicans, gave a reason for what they did, pointing out that trees had such and such an effect on climate—the whole in plain clear terms and printed in the Arabic script.

STORY OF THE DETERMINIST

There was, however, a Mohammedan who, on reading this, immediately saw in it an advertisement of wealth and pasture. He drove his goats for nearly fifteen miles, camped outside the wall, and next day lifted each animal carefully one by one into the enclosure that they might browse upon the tender shoots of the young trees. "Better," he thought, "that my goats should fatten than that the mad Christians should enjoy this tree-fad of theirs which is of no advantage to God or man."

When his last goat was over two rangers came, and, in extreme anger, brought him before the magistrate, where he was asked what reason he could give for the wrong thing he had done. He answered, "*R'aho*, it was the will of God. *Mektoub*, it was written"— or words to that effect.

* * * * *

The platform of the Rock of Cirta is the place from which the effort of the French

CIRTA OR CONSTANTINE

over all this land can best be judged, for it is the centre round which nature and history have grouped the four changes of Barbary. The rock is like those headlands which jut out from inland ranges and dominate deep harbours; it is as bold as are such capes, and is united, as they are, with the mass of land behind it by a neck of even surface—the only passage by which the rock itself can be approached. On every side but this, very sharp slopes of grass, broken by precipices, plunge down in a mountainous way to the valleys, and at the foot of the most sheer of these there tumbles noisily in a profound gorge the torrent called Rummel, that is, "The Tawny," for it is as yellow as a lion or as sea-sand.

The trench is so deep and dark that one may stand above it towards evening and hear the noise of the water and yet see no gleam of light reflected from it, it runs so far below. It is this stream which has made on the Rock of Cirta (though it is out of the true Tell and far into the Tableland) a habitable fortress and a town; the town called Constantine.

Such sites are very rare. Luxemburg is one, a stronghold cut off by similar precipitous valleys. Jerusalem is another. Wherever they are found the origin of their fortress goes back beyond the beginning of history, they are tribal, and their record is principally of war. So it is with Cirta. The legends of the nomads say that they descended from some enormous dusky figure, a God of the Atlas and of Spain —a giant God marching along the shores of the ocean followed perpetually by armies. Even this first of African names was mixed up with Cirta, for the title of the rock was that of his loves, and the name Cirta given it by these horsemen of Numidia was the name of their universal mother. A man can be certain, as he walks along the edges of the place to-day and looks down into the gulfs below it, that men have so moved here amid buildings and in a fixed town with altars and a name ever since first they knew how to mortar stones together and to obey laws. The close pack of houses standing thus apart upon a peak has in it, therefore, something consistently sacred. Permanence and continuity are to be discovered here only among the cities of Africa ; and its landscape and character of themselves impress the traveller with a certitude that here will be planted on into time the capital of

Constantine

the native blood: too far removed from the sea for colonisation or piracy to destroy it: too well cut off by those trenches of defence to be sacked and overrun: too peopled and well watered to decay. The town has been taken in every conquest, and every conqueror has boasted himself to have overcome the walls of rock, the hundreds of feet of sheer climbing. The boast is manifestly absurd, though the temptation to make it was irresistible. When Cirta has

CONSTANTINE

been stormed only one gate admitted the invaders, and that was the isthmus which leads from the platform of the summit to the tableland beyond. It was here that Massinissa and here that the Romans entered. By this entry came the French soldiers, and the market which stands there is called to-day "The Place of the Breach."

There is a place in Constantine where the full history of the town is best felt, and that is in the new Town Hall, which stands upon the edge of the rock upon the side furthest from the river and looks at the storms blowing over the uplands from Atlas and driving low clouds right at the crest of the walls. In this building are preserved (in no great number) the antiquities of the place and its neighbourhood. Here is a little silver victory which once fluttered, it is thought, in the hand of that great statue which adorned the Capitol, and here are long rows of tombs

The Inscriptions

from the beginning of the Italian influence till the time of the martyrs : you see carved upon them the slow change of the mind until the last of the pagans boast of such virtues and have already that sort of content which the acceptation of the creed was to bequeath to succeeding time. This record of the epitaphs, though brief, is perfect; you watch at work in them the spirit that made St. Cyprian transforming the African soil; but their chief interest is in this, that they are, as it were, a rediscovery of ourselves. You dig through centuries of alien rubbish overlying the Roman dead, and, when you have dug deeply enough you come suddenly upon Europe. For twelve hundred years an idiom quite unfamiliar to us has alone been spoken here : beneath it you find the august and reasonable Latin, and as you read you feel about you the air of home. For all those generations the manifold aspect of the divine was forgotten : there were

The Inscriptions

no shrines nor priests to rear them. Then, deep down, you discover a tablet upon a tomb, and, reading it, you find it was carved in memory of a priestess of Isis who was so gracious and who so served the divinities of the woods that when she died *ingemuerunt Dryades :* twice I read those delicate words, delicately chiselled in hard stone, and I saw her going in black, with her head bent, through groves. A trace of colouring remains upon the lettering of the verse and a powerful affection lingers in it, so that the past is preserved. Islam destroyed with fanaticism the figures of animals and of men : here in these European carvings they are everywhere. The barbarian creed conceived or implanted a barbaric fear of vines : here you see Bacchus, young, on the corner of a frieze, and gentle old Silenus carried heavily along.

* * * * *

If it is from the Rock of Cirta, from Constantine, that the recovery of the province

Cæsarea or Cherchel

and its re-entry into Europe is best perceived —for there stands the unchanging centre of Africa, and there can all the threads of her destiny be grasped—yet there is another place far westward and down upon the shore, where the wound that Europe suffered by the Mohammedan invasion is more marked and long eclipse of our race more apparent. It is the Bay of Cæsarea.

Constantine is so necessary to Africa that its very name (and it is alone in this among all the cities) has been preserved. Cæsarea has lost its name and its dignity too. The Barbarians have come to call her "Cherchel": as for her rank, it has been forgotten altogether; yet this port was for a hundred years peculiar among all others in the Mediterranean—it was more remote, more splendid, and more new. The accident which created it lent a great story to its dynasty, and its situation here, along the steeper shores that lead on to the Straits and to the outer ocean, lent some western mystery to it and some appeal.

Cleopatra, the Queen of Egypt, was famous throughout the Mediterranean for her beauty. The last of her lovers—it is well known—was Anthony the Triumvir, who had desired (until he saw her) to inherit from Cæsar and to rule the whole world. This ambition he abandoned after one battle, lost, it is said, through her folly; and soon after that defeat they chose to die. But a fruit of their loves, and a picture, perhaps, of his courage and of her magnificence, survived in a daughter whom her mother had dedicated to the Moon and had called Selene. This child was married out into Barbary, to the king of the nomads, and here, in Cherchel, she held with her husband for many years a court which gathered round it the handicraft of Corinth, the letters of Athens, and some reflected splendour from the town of Rome.

He was of those horsemen who had now

Cherchel

for two centuries served Carthage as mercenaries or Rome as allies. To the cities of the sea coast, which were Italian or Asiatic in blood, these riders of the uplands had been outer men. They appeared barbaric to the end, and, at the very end, it was their blood, perhaps, that rebelled against the tradition of order and that joined first the Vandal and then the Arab. The king was dark and a barbarian. This wife who was sent to him inherited the broad forehead of Rome and the silence of Egypt, and was also an heiress to the generals of Alexander. There met in her, therefore, all those high sources from whose unison Christendom has proceeded. She came west to a new land that did not know cut stone and hardly roads : in a little time she had built a city.

By some economic power which no one has explained, but which may be compared to the wealth of our smaller independent States to-day and their merchants, to Antwerp

CHERCHEL

or to The Hague, this city of Mauretania rose to be a marvel. The porticos stretched along that rise of land, and a mile of new work, columns and pedestalled statues and arcades, looked down from the slope and saw, making for the shore, perpetual sails from the eastward. Great libraries dignified the city: a complete security and a humane consideration for the arts continually increased its glory. The passion for scholarship, which was at that time excessive, may have touched the palace here with something of the ridiculous. The king wrote, dictated, or commanded a whole shelf of books and was eager for the pride of authorship. But no other note of indignity entered their State, and all around them, looking out to sea, was a resurrection of Greece.

This queen and her husband lived on into old age thus, untroubled in their isolation and their content, and destined (as they thought) to leave a dynasty which even the

Cherchel

domination of Rome would protect and spare.

Nothing is left. Rome seized their town at last. Their descendants perished. All Mauretania was compelled to follow the common line of unity. For four hundred years it has no history save that under the Roman order it endured and increased. The Vandals passed it by : it might still stand had there not fallen upon it the Mohammedan invasion which everywhere destroyed, or rather abandoned, a Roman endeavour. The neglect which was native to the Arab, the sharp breach which he made in tradition, ended Cæsarea. To-day, a little market town, a tenth of the old capital, barrenly preserves a memory of those two thousand years. A few fragments which the plough recovers or which the builders have spared are gathered in one place : the rest is parched fields and trees.

One conspicuous monument survives to emphasise the retreat of the empire. It is

The Aqueduct

something the Arab could not waste because it did not lie within the circuit of the walls: its great stones were too remote from his buildings to be removed, and its mass too threatening to be undermined. It was the Aqueduct. This, for the most part, still stands, and carries an aspect of endurance which is the more awful in that nothing else of the city

The Aqueduct

has endured. It spans a lonely valley in which the bay and the old harbour are forgotten, and it is as enormous as the name of Rome.

It is more like a wall for height and completeness than are any of the huge Roman arches I know. Its height is such that it catches the mind more strongly than does the Pont du Gard, and its completeness such that it arrests the eye more than do the long trails of arches that stretch like rays across the Campagna. It appalls one because it is quite alone, and because the multitude that gave it a meaning has disappeared. One could wish to have seen this thing before the French came, when the brushwood of the valley was quite deserted and when one might have thought it fixed for ever in an intangible isolation which no European would come again to reoccupy and to disturb.

Even to-day one may climb to the further, inland, side and look down the perspective

THE AQUEDUCT

of its arches with some illusion of loneliness, and live for an hour in the fifteen centuries of its abandonment. Its height, its fineness, and the ruin of its use are so best seen, and its long line of purpose, pointing on to a city that no longer remembers baths or fountains. It is the ceaseless refrain of Africa. Italy, Gaul, and Spain have ruins like these, but these ruins are right against a life which has always been vigorous and to-day is especially renewed : only in this one province of Africa do you find Rome arrested, as it were—its spirit caught away and its body turned into stone.

* * * * *

There was last to be seen, before I could leave this province, the desert and those dead towns which stand along the hither fringe of it: the deserted homes of the Romans, and chief among them Timgad.

The Atlas, I had heard, is there at its highest, and the knot of mountains into which it rises is called the Aurès. Upon its southern side it fell steeply (I was told) upon the Sahara, and its northern supported, on the last of the High Table-land, those ruined cities. Here the frontier legionaries had been posted, and here the Arab invasion had so wasted the forests and dried up the run of water that the towns had died at once. This Timgad in particular is famous for its perfection and for the complete survival of its form, but especially for this, that you walk along paved streets and between standing columns and look, from the seats of a theatre, towards a great arch or gate not yet fallen, and yet never hear the voice of a living man.

I took my way to this place, the last

Journey to the Desert

of the towns I desired to see—the tombstone, as it were, of the empire, the symbol or promise of the reconquest. I went partly by day and partly by night, partly by the railroad and partly on foot across the High Plateau southward till I should come to it. Upon my way I met many men who should, perhaps, have no part in such a little historical essay as is this, but for fear I should altogether forget them I will write them down.

The first was an ill-dressed fellow, young, and with very sad eyes such as men keep sometimes in early life but lose at last as they learn in time to prey upon others. He had been unfortunate. We went along together across a plain peculiarly lonely, and towards a large, bare, isolated rock as high as a Welsh mountain and, as it seemed, quite uninhabited. We were already in sight of the main range of Atlas, and in the far ravines was a darkness that might, perhaps, be made by cedar-trees, but all around us was nothing but bare land

Story of the Lions

and now and then a glint from salt marshes far away.

I asked him from what part of France he had come. He answered that he was born in the colony. Then I asked him whether the colonists thought themselves prosperous or no. He said, as do all sad people, that luck was the difference. Those whom fortune loved, prospered; those whom she hated, failed. He was right; but when he came to examples he was startling. He showed me, high upon the rock before us, which I had thought quite lonely, a considerable building, made of the stones of the place and in colour similar to the mountain itself. "Beyond this hill," he said, "is Batna, and beyond Batna is Lambèse. Since you are walking to Timgad you will pass both these places, and everywhere you will hear of the House of the Lions. Then you will learn, if ever you needed proof, that it is luck which governs all our efforts in this colony." I looked

Story of the Lions

curiously at the great house, and asked him to tell me the story. This he did; and I write here, as exactly as I can from memory, the story he told.

"In that very place upon the hillside where now stands so huge a house stood, when we were yet children, a little hut of stone such as the settlers build, with two rooms in it only, a bed, three chairs, a table, and a cooking-pot. And to this poverty nothing was added, for ill-luck pursued that roof.

"There lived under it a man and his wife who had two children. They had come here to rise with the country (as it is said), but, instead of so rising, first one evil and then another fell upon them till their little horde was eaten up and the field also, and the man had to work for others—a most miserable fate. He got work in the building of the prison of Lambèse, but, as he was not created by God to be a merchant or a mortar-mixer,

Story of the Lions

nor even a carrier of stone, he earned very little and was always in dread of being sent away; and his companions jeered at him, for the unfortunate are ridiculous not only among the rich, but in every rank; and not only the rich jeer at poverty and shun it, but the poor also—indeed, all men.

"In a word, this man was in so miserable a way that at last he took to following his wife to church and to having recourse to shrines, as do many men when their afflictions are unendurable, and among other shrines he went to that called 'St. Anthony of the Lion.' Now, though it is ridiculous to believe that the Lion there helped him, (for it is not a saint,) yet good came to him through Lions.

"One day, when he had gone off to work with a heavy heart, leaving in the house but one five-franc piece, his wife, who was now all soured by misfortune and was wearied out with ceaseless work, heard a single knock at the door, and when she went to it she found

Story of the Lions

a nomad boy of the desert from beyond Aurès, who held in his arms two little cubs with soft feet and peering eyes who were mewing for their mother: they were the cubs of Lions.

"The Arab boy, who was dark, erect, and strong, said, 'God sends you these. They are five francs.' She answered, 'God be with you. I cannot pay.' When, however, he made to go away silently, without bargaining, she said, 'God forgive me, but I will buy them'; for she thought to herself, 'perhaps I can sell them again for more,' for Lions are rare and wonderful beasts. So she took her five-franc piece from beneath a leaden statue of St. Anthony in the window, and she paid the Arab boy from beyond Aurès, from the Sahara, and she said, 'God save you, the lioness will follow the scent'; and he said, 'God will overshadow me,' and went gravely away, biting the five-franc piece to see if it was good.

Story of the Lions

"Now, when her husband came home they decided to go into Batna and sell the cubs, but their children, for whom they could afford no sort of toy, were already so fond of the little beasts that they had not the heart to sell them: they skimped and starved and ran into debt, but as the love of these Lions increased in their hearts the more determined were they to keep them; and they used to say, 'God will provide,' and other things of that sort.

"The cubs, then, grew to be the size of spaniels, and then they became grown and were the size of hounds, and soon manes grew on them and they were the size of St. Bernards, and their eyes grew bright and shone at evening; and at last they were perfect Lions. But from a long association with Christian men they were genial, decorous, and loving, and ate nothing but cooked meat, bread, and now and then a sweetmeat. Also, they could stand up and beg. They could roar at com-

Story of the Lions

mand. They could jump over each other's backs; they could play as many tricks as a dog. It was in this way that good came from them.

"For one day, when this man and his wife were in a better mood and had forgotten their poverty for an hour, there came to them in the carrier's cart a parcel of wine sent them by a relative who had a vineyard. This may have been the turning of their luck: one cannot tell. Luck is above mankind. But, anyhow, they asked the carrier in and gave him wine. Now the carrier was a Mohammedan, and Mohammedans are treacherous, so when he saw two Lions walking about in a lonely house he did not call it witchcraft, as would a Christian man, but at once he offered a price for them; but the man and his wife had hearts so good they would not sell. Then the carrier changed his tune, and offered to hire them for one week and to pay for this fifty francs: this they gladly accepted. For the carrier and men like him are incapable of honour except in one small thing, which is the keeping of words and dates: in this they are most exact. So at the end of the week he brought back the Lions, and gave the man and his wife fifty francs.

"But more was to come. For the carrier (and men like him) see profit where a Christian man would not see it, and he made a proposition to these people. He said: 'Your Lions jump through hoops, they beg for sugar, and do other entertaining things: now I will travel with you and them, and half of all we earn shall go to you.' The man and his wife were so simple and so necessitous that they accepted, and the tour began. But That Which Watches Over Us at last rewarded the man and his wife, for within a week the carrier died, and they went on up and down the country by themselves with their children, showing the Lions, till they began to earn

Story of the Lions

incredible sums. They went to the great towns and to the sea coast. At last they became so rich that they went to Algiers, and there it is, as you may imagine, large rents but larger earnings. They lived in Algiers for one year, and became at last so rich that they crossed the sea and showed their Lions in Provence, in Lyons, and would have shown them in Paris but that, by the time they reached Tournus, they came to their own people and found themselves rich enough. There the man and his wife remained, but their children, who had been born in Africa, came back, and here they are now. They have friends to dinner every day, and all on account of Lions."

When he had done this story he added, "It is true." Then we went on to Batna together without a word, but when we reached Batna we had dinner together and spoke of many other things, but I have space for

The Bargaining at Batna

nothing except this story of his about the lions.

* * * * *

Having arrived at Batna, which is the starting-place for Timgad and also for the desert beyond, I found that there was a good road which the French had built going along a valley under Aurès, but that the distance was over twenty miles. I wasted the daylight bargaining, for no one would drive me twenty miles for less than sixteen shillings. It was late, and in my eagerness to bargain I missed the chance of a day-light march, for it was within an hour of sunset when the night driver who was to start on the Tebessa road (which runs near Timgad) a little later refused me. The poorer people whom I asked told me that no one else was going eastward along that lonely valley, but that, if I were to reach Timgad, I must make a night march of it or wait a night over in Batna itself at an inn.

Adventure is never to be refused, so I

Lamboesis

went out eastward alone under the evening, and I was well rewarded, though I went hungry for hours and was afoot nearly all the way, for I saw a great sight under the sunset, and I met a man I shall never meet again.

The sight I saw was Lambèse, which was called Lamboesis by the Romans, and this is what stamps it upon the mind of a lonely man before nightfall : not what remains, for hardly anything remains, but that the fragments which remain of it should be so far apart.

There is a sort of long cup or hollow here pointing at a spur of the Atlas—that high mountain which holds up the sky. The big lift of Aurès is on one side of this hollow, mixing into the clouds, and on the other are isolated and uninhabited high hills. The very floor of this valley is as high as the top of Cader Idris is in Wales ; the heights beyond are as high as the Pyrenees ; and an air of

The Praetorian Tower

desertion haunts the place. It is impossible to forget that the Sahara is near by, down beyond the crest of the range. For though the land is muddy and the sky full of rough clouds and rain, yet the rain seems to make no grass and the land is bare. In such a world there stands up before one a square and hardly ruined tower.

A man of northern Europe looking at this thing from the high road cannot but think it Jacobean (if he is English) or (if he is German or French) a thing of the Thirty Years' War. It might be later perhaps, the freak of some Highland landlord or the relic of some local rebellion. It is older than our language by far, and almost older than the Faith. As one looks at it one cannot feel but only know its age, and one watches it up an avenue of stones wondering why it stands so lonely. But one's wonder has no stuff in it till one goes on half a mile and more: by the roadside is a pile of Roman

The Vastness of Lambèse

stones. These also stood in Lamboesis. Then, feeling himself yet within the walls of an unseen city, a man looks back over the stretch he has come and is appalled. In such a gaze you look westward towards the light beyond the mountains. The valley is already dark. The high road which the French have made glistens as hard as stone under the last light. Trees are still visible, especially the few mournful and hard pyramids of the cypress, but the little village, the modern prison (for there is a prison), and the rare labourers here and there are muffled up in twilight; and there lies before one a mere emptiness, beyond which, a long way off, dwindled to quite little, is the Praetorian Tower. A sharp memory of childhood from beyond years of common experience so strikes the mind.

The spread plain with its one central tower seems infinite; it is now without hedges or trees or roofs or men; but once the Legion had filled up everything.

The Driver Passes

It was all quite bare as I surveyed it—more bare than a heath or a down, and as large as any landscape you may know.

While I was watching this empty space, and surmising what contrast it would make with the famous and crowded ruins of Timgad to which this Lamboesis had been a neighbouring city, as Chichester is to Arundel—or, better still, as Portsmouth and its armament is to Southampton and its trade—I heard the rumble of heavy and fast wheels, and a man driving a coach passed me and then pulled up at my hail. He was the same man who had refused my bargain an hour and more before. He was driving the night coach to Tebessa. Not understanding men, he raised his price. I told him that I would pay him only what I had offered at Batna, *less* the price of the miles I had gone. He would not yield, but he did these three things: first, he promised to send word, as he passed, to an old Soldier who kept a house near

The Cold

Timgad that a traveller was on the road; secondly, he gave me advice, telling me that I should freeze to death by night in that valley (for it was growing cold and the weather would not hold under such a sky); thirdly, he informed me of the exact distance, which was at the thirty-second stone, where there is a branch road to the right, leading in half an hour up the slopes of the range to Timgad. Then he drove on, and I spent what was left of a doubtful light in pressing onwards.

*   *   *   *   *

A great mass of snow had recently covered the peaks, and in the valley up which I was trudging freezing gusts and very sharp scurries of cold rain disturbed the traveller. I had already passed the last ruins of the Romans and had seen, far off in the dusk, the last arch of the Legions standing all alone with one big tree beside it. The west was wild-red under the storm, and it was cut like a fret

The Arab

with the jagged edge of the Sierras, quite black, when I saw against the purple of a nearer hill the white cloak of an Arab.

He drove a little cart—a light cart with two wheels. His horse was of such a sort as you may buy any day in Africa for ten

pounds, that is, it was gentle, strong, swift, and small, and looked in the half-light as though it did not weigh upon the earth but as though it were accustomed to running over the tops of the sea. I said to the Arab: " Will you not give me a lift ? " He answered : " If it the will of God." Hearing so excellent an answer, and finding myself a

The Arab

part of universal fate, I leapt into his cart and he drove along through the gloaming, and as he went he sang a little song which had but three notes in it, and each of these notes was divided from the next by only a quarter of a note. So he sang, and so I sat by his side.

At last he saw that it was only right to break into talk, if for no other reason than that I was his guest; so he said quite suddenly, looking straight before him:

"I am very rich."

"I," said I, "am moderately poor."

At this he shook his head and said: "I am more fortunate than you; I am very, very rich." He then wagged his head again slowly from side to side and was silent for a good minute or more.

He next said slyly, with a mixture of curiosity and politeness: "My Lord, when you say you are poor you mean poor after the manner of the Romans, that is, with no

The Arab

money in your pocket but always the power to obtain it."

"No," said I, "I have no land, and not even the power of which you speak. I am really, though moderately, poor. All that I get I earn by talking in public places in the cold weather, and in spring time and summer by writing and by other tricks." He looked solemn for a moment, and then said: "Have you, indeed, no land?" I said "No" again; for at that moment I had none. Then he replied: "I have sixteen hundred acres of land."

When he had said this he tossed back his head in that lion-like way they have, for they are as theatrical as children or animals, and he went on: "Yes, and of these one-fourth is in good fruit-trees . . . they bear . . . they bear . . . I cannot contain myself for well-being." "God give you increase," said I. "A good word," said he, "and I would say the same to you but that you have nothing

THE ARAB

to increase with. However, it is the will of God. ' To one man it comes, from another it goes,' said the Barber, and again it is said, ' Which of you can be certain ? ' "

These last phrases he rattled off like a lesson with no sort of unction : it was evidently a form. He then continued :

" I have little rivulets running by my trees. He - from - whom - I - bought had let them go dry; I nurtured them till they sparkled. They feed the roots of my orchard. I am very rich. Some let their walls fall down ; I prop them up; nay, sometimes I rebuild. All my roofs are tiled with tiles from Marseilles. . . . I am very rich." Then I took up the psalm in my turn, and I said :

" What is it to be rich if you are not also famous ? Can you sing or dance or make men laugh or cry by your recitals ? I will not ask if you can draw or sculpture, for your religion forbids it, but do you play

The Arab

the instrument or the flute? Can you put together wise phrases which are repeated by others?"

To this he answered quite readily: "I have not yet attempted to do any of these things you mention: doubtless were I to try them I should succeed, for I have become very rich, and a man who is rich in money from his own labour could have made himself rich in any other thing."

When he said this I appreciated from whence such a doctrine had invaded England. It had come from the Orientals. I listened to him as he went on: "But it is no matter; my farm is enough for me. If there were no men with farms, who would pay for the flute and the instrument and the wise beggar and the rest? Ah! who would feed them?"

"None," said I, "you are quite right." So we went quickly forward for a long time under the darkness, saying nothing more

The Arab

until a thought moved him. "My father was rich," he said, "but I am far richer than my father."

It was cold, and I remembered what a terrible way I had to go that night—twenty miles or more through this empty land of Africa. So I was shivering as I answered: "Your father did well in his day, and through him you are rich. It says, 'Revere your father: God is not more to you.'" He answered: "You speak sensibly; I have sons." Then for some time more we rode along upon the high wheels.

But in a few minutes the lights of a low steading appeared far off under poplar-trees, and as he waved his hand towards it he said: "That is my farm." "Blessed be your farm," said I, "and all who dwell in it." To this he made the astonishing reply: "God will give it to you; I have none." "What is that you say?" I asked him in amazement. He repeated the phrase, and then I saw that it

The Arab

was a form, and that it was of no importance whether I understood it or not. But I understood the next thing which he said as he stopped at his gates, which was: " Here, then, you get out." I asked him what I should pay for the service, and he replied: " What you will. Nothing at all." So I gave him a franc, which was all I had in silver. He took it with a magnificent salutation, saying as he did so : " I can accept nothing from you," which, I take it, was again a form. Then the night swallowed him up, and I shall never see him again till that Great Day in which we both believed but of which neither of us could know anything at all.

* * * * *

We were born, I cannot tell how many leagues apart, in different climates and for different destinies, but we were two men together in the night, and, for a short time, we were very near each other compared with

The Goat-Story again

the distance of the stars, or with the distance that separates any two philosophers.

* * * * *

Many who read this will say they know the Mohammedan better than I. They will be right: then let them explain the story of the goats, for I cannot. I will repeat it to save them the trouble of turning back.

A young man of Ain-Yagout, hearing that the Government had carefully planted little cedars on a distant hill, drove his goats fifteen miles to browse upon the same. "Better," said he, "that I should flourish than the Government, and that my goats should give milk than that these silly little trees should fatten."

They caught him and brought him before the magistrate, where he confessed what he had done, and even that he had lifted the goats laboriously, one by one, over a high wall to get at the Government trees. But when they asked him what good reason he could give for his conduct, he replied:

The Moor

" *R'aho!* It was the will of God. *Mektoub*, it was written."

Or words to that effect.

I will admit that when the full lips, the long uncertain eye and the tall forehead of the true Arab met me in these short travels I was always half silenced and half moved to question and to learn. But I saw such Oriental features rarely, for, in spite of the turban and the bernous, they are very rare.

Indeed, of all the men I came across in this country, only two were of the purely Oriental kind the books make out to be so common. One was a fierce Moor of gigantic stature and incredible girth. He was dressed in bright green, and drank the cordial called *crême de menthe* in a little bower. The other was a poor Arab and old, who sold fruits upon a stall in Setif. In his face there was a deep contempt of Christendom.

The snow fell all around him swiftly, mixed with sleet and sharp needles of cold

The Little Old Semite

rain. It was evening and the people were passing down the street hurriedly to find their homes: so passed I, when I saw him standing like a little stunted ghost in the rain. He knew me at once for some one to whom Africa was strange, and therefore might have hoped to make me stop even upon such a night to buy of him. Yet he did not say a word, but only looked at me as much as to say: "Fool! will you buy?" And I looked back at him as I passed, and put my answer into my eyes as much as to say: "No! Barbarian, I will not buy." In this way we met and parted, and we shall never see each other again till that Great Day . . .

* * * * *

Remembering him and this last one who had given me a ride, I went on through the night towards Timgad.

The Lonely Night March

It was a very lonely road.

Loneliness, when it is absolute, is very difficult to depict, for it is a negation and lacks quality, and therefore words fail it. But one may express the loneliness of that valley best by saying that it felt, not as though men had deserted it, but as though men had perpetually tried to return to it and, as perpetually, had despaired and left the sullen earth. The impression was false. The Romans had once thoroughly possessed and tilled this land: the scrub had once been forests, the shifting soil ordered and bounded fields; but the Mohammedan sterility had sunk in so deeply that one could not believe that our people had ever been here. Even the sharp and recent memory of those ruins of Lamboesis faded in the stillness. Europe came back into my mind. The full rivers and the fields which are to us a natural landscape are but a made garden and are due to continuous tradition, and I wondered whether,

The Lonely Night March

if that tradition were finally lost, our sons would come to see, in England as I saw here in the night in Africa, vague hills without trees and drifts of mould and sand through which the rain-bursts would dig deep channels at random.

There was a moon risen by this time, but it lay behind a level flow of clouds. All along the way, to my right, made smaller by the darkness, lay Aurès—one could still just discern the snow upon his summits. The road went on—French, exact, and, if I may say so, alien—bridging this barbaric void which already smelt of the desert where it lay beyond those mountains down under the southern wall of Atlas. For the desert, when I had seen Timgad, I determined to strike.

So the road went on, and I with it till I came to the thirty-second stone, and recognised its number by holding a match close by. Then I knew that I had covered twenty miles and was close to Timgad. A branch road

The Columns of Timgad

opened out on the right, and there was a sign-post pointing along it. I followed the new road across a careful girder bridge such as might cross a brook in Normandy. I saw a light up on the rise of the foot-hills, and beyond it, suddenly and yet dimly, a very mob of columns. They stood up against the vague glimmer of the sky of every size and in thousands, as though they were marching. A little rift in the clouds let in the moon upon them palely. Her light was soon extinguished, but in that moment I had seen a large city, unroofed and dead, in the middle of this wasted land.

However men may act who see a vision but see it in extreme fatigue, so did I. I suffered the violent impression of that ghost, but my curiosity was no longer of the body. I took no step to see the wonder which this gleam had hinted at, but I turned and struck at the door of the house which was now quite near me, and which was still lit within. An

The Old Soldier

old man, small, bent, and full of energy, opened the door to me. He was that soldier of whom they had told me at Lambèse.

"I was expecting you," he said.

I remembered that the driver had promised to warn him, and I was grateful.

"I have prepared you a meal," he went on. Then, after a little hesitation, "It is mutton: it is neither hot nor cold."

A man who has been on guard as often as had this old sergeant need not mind awakening in the small hours, and a man who has marched twenty miles and more in the dark must eat what he is given, though it be sheep and tepid. So I sat down. He brought me their very rough African wine and a loaf, and sat down opposite me, looking at me fixedly under the candle. Then he said:

"To-morrow you will see Timgad, which is the most wonderful town in the world."

"Certainly not to-night," I answered; to which he said, "No!"

The Strange Food

I took a bite of the food, and he at once continued rapidly: "Timgad is a marvel. We call it 'the marvel.' I had thought of calling this house 'Timgad the Marvel,' or, again, 'Timgad the——.'"

"Is this sheep?" I said.

"Certainly," he answered. "What else could it be but sheep?"

"Good Lord!" I said, "it might be anything. There is no lack of beasts on God's earth." I took another bite and found it horrible.

"I desire you to tell me frankly," said I, "whether this is goat. There are many Italians in Africa, and I shall not blame any man for giving me goat's flesh. The Hebrew prophets ate it and the Romans; only tell me the truth, for goat is bad for me."

He said it was not goat. Indeed, I believed him, for it was of a large and terrible sort, as though it had roamed the hills and towered above all goats and sheep. I thought

The Strange Food

of lions, but remembered that their value would forbid their being killed for the table. I again attempted the meal, and he again began:

"Timgad is a place——"

At this moment a god inspired me, and I shouted, "Camel!" He did not turn a hair. I put down my knife and fork, and pushed the plate away. I said:

"You are not to be blamed for giving me the food of the country, but for passing it under another name."

He was a good host, and did not answer. He went out, and came back with cheese. Then he said, as he put it down before me:

"I do assure you it is sheep," and we discussed the point no more.

But in the hour that followed we spoke of many things—of the army (which he remembered), of active service (which he regretted, for he had lost half a hand), of money (which he loved), and of the Church—which he hated. He was good to the bottom of his soul. His face was sad. He had most evidently helped the poor, he had fought hard and gained his independence, and there he was under Aurès, in a neglected place a thousand miles away from his own people talking French talk of disestablishment and of the equality of all opinion before the law. So we talked till the camel (or sheep) was stiff in its plate and cold, and the first glimmer of dawn had begun to sadden the bare room and to oppress the yellow light of the candle. Then he took me to a room, and as I went I saw from a window, beyond a garden he had planted, the awful sight of Timgad, utterly silent and ruined, stretching a mile under the dull morning; and with that sight still controlling me I fell heavily asleep.

When the morning came I looked out again from my window and I saw the last of the storm still hurrying overhead, and beneath and before me, of one even grey colour and quite silent, the city of Timgad. There

Timgad

was no one in it alive. There were no roofs and no criers. It was all ruins standing up everywhere: broken walls and broken columns absolutely still, except in one place where some pious care had led the water back to its old channels. There a little fountain ran from an urn that a Cupid held.

I passed at once through the gates and walked for perhaps an hour, noting curiously

a hundred things: the shop-stalls and the lines of pedestals; the flag-stones of the Forum and the courses of brick—even, small, Roman and abandoned. I walked so, gazing

Timgad

sometimes beyond the distant limits of the city to the distant slopes of Atlas, till I came to a high place where the Theatre had once stood, dug out of a hillside and built in with rows of stone seats. Here I sat down to draw the stretch of silence before me, and then I recognised for the first time that I was very tired.

I said to myself: "This comes of my long march through the night"; but when I had finished my drawing and had got up to walk again (for one might walk in Timgad for many days, or for a lifetime if one chose) I found a better reason for my fatigue, which was this: that, try as I would I could not walk firmly and strongly upon those deserted streets or across the flags of that Forum, but I was compelled by something in the town to tread uncertainly and gently. When I recollected myself I would force my feet to a natural and ready step; but in a moment, as my thoughts were taken by some new

Timgad

aspect of the place, I found myself walking again with strain and care, noiselessly, as one does in shrines, or in the room of a sleeper or of the dead. It was not I that did it, but the town.

I saw, some hundred yards away, a man going to his field along a street of Timgad: he showed plainly for the houses had sunk to rubble upon either side of his way. This was the first life I had seen under that stormy mountain morning, and in that lonely place which had been lonely for so very long. He also walked doubtfully and with careful feet; he looked downward and made no sound.

I went up and down Timgad all that morning. The sun was not high before I felt that by long wandering between the columns and peering round many corners and finding nothing, one at last became free of the city. An ease and a familiarity, a sort of friendship with abandoned but

Timgad

once human walls, took the traveller as he grew used to the silence; but whether in such companionship he did not suffer some evil influence, I cannot say.

I came to one place and to another and to another, each quite without men, and each casting such an increasing spell upon the mind as is cast by voices heard in the night, when one does not know whether they are of the world, or not of the world.

I came to a triumphal arch which had once guarded the main entry to the city from Lamboesis and the west. It was ornate, four-sided, built, one would think, in the centuries of the decline. Beyond it, the suburbs into which the city expanded just before it fell stretched far out into the plain. Not far from it a very careful inscription recalled a man who has thus survived as he wished to survive; the sacred tablet testified to the spirit which unites the religion of antiquity with our own—for it was chiselled in

Timgad

fulfilment of a vow. In another place was the statue of the gods' mother, crowned with a wall and towers. This also was of the decline, but still full of that serenity which faces wore before the Barbarian march and the sack of cities.

There is a crossing of the streets in Timgad where one may sit a long time and consider her desolation upon every side. The seclusion is absolute, and the presence of so many made things with none to use them gradually invades the mind. The sun gives life to you as you look down this Decumanian way, and see the runnels

Timgad

where the wheels ran once noisily to the market; it warms you but it nourishes for

you no companions. The town stares at you and is blind.

Against the sky, upon a little mound, stand

Timgad

two tall columns, much taller than the rest. They shine under the low winter sun from every part of Timgad and are white over the plain of grey stones. They may have been raised for the Temple of Capitoline Jove.

These will detain the traveller for as long as he may choose to regard them, so violently do they impress him with the negation of time. It is said that in certain abnormal moods things infinitely great and infinitely little are present together in the mind: that vast spaces of the imagination and minute contacts of the finger-tips are each figured in the brain, the one not driving out the other. In such moods (it is said) proportion and reality grow faint, and the unity and poise of our limited human powers are in peril. Into such a mood is a man thrown by Timgad, and especially by these two pillars of white stone. They proceed so plainly from the high conceptions of man: so much were their sculptors what we are in every

TIMGAD

western character : so fully do they satisfy us : so recent and clean is the mark of the tool upon them that they fill a man with society and leave him ready to meet at once a living city full of his fellows. It only needs a spoken word or the clack of a sandal to be back into the moment when all these things were alive. And meanwhile, with that impression overpowering one's sense, there, physically present, is a desolation so complete that measure fails it. No oxen moving : no smoke : no roof among the rare trees of the horizon : no gleam of water and no sound. It is as though not certain centuries but an incalculable space of days coexisted with the present, and as though, for one eternal moment, a vision of the absolute in which time is not were permitted—for no good—to the yet embodied soul.

I do not know what was the hour in which I turned and left this sight, and leaving by the southern gate made for the mountain

The Stranger

range of Aurès. But it was yet early afternoon, and the track had risen but little into the hills when I saw, some little way off, seated upon a great squared stone which had lain there since the departure of our people, a man of a kind I had not met in Africa before.

By his dress he was rather a colonist than a native, for he wore no turban—indeed his head was bare; but his long cloak was cut in an unusual shape, covering him almost entirely; it was dark and made of some stuff that had certainly not been woven in a modern loom. He saluted me as I came.

When I approached him and saluted him in return, his face could be seen inspired with a peculiar power, which, at a distance, his attitude alone had discovered. It was not easy to be sure whether its lines were drawn from Italy or from those rare exceptions wherein the east seems sometimes to surpass our own race in force and dignity. His forehead was low and very broad, his hair short, crisp, strong, and of the colour of steel ; his lips, which were thin and controlled, had in their firm outline something of a high sadness, and his whole features recalled those which tradition gives to the makers and destroyers of religions. But it was his eyes that gave him so singular and (as I can still believe though the adventure is now long past) so magical an influence. These were in colour like the sea in March, grey-green and full of light, or like some mountain stones which when they are polished show the same translucent and natural hue, shining from within with vivid changes ; but, much more than their luminous colour, their expression arrested me, for it had in it an experience of immense horizons, and resembled that which may sometimes be caught in the eyes of birds who have seen the earth from the heights of the sky.

I first spoke and asked him whether I

The Stranger

was well upon the path that would lead me under Aurès, through the pass, to the sandstone hills from whose summits one could see the desert for which I was bound.

Whether Timgad had disturbed me, or his speech had in it that something which at the time I feared, I cannot tell; but the very short dialogue we had together influenced me in my loneliness for a whole day, as a vivid dream will do. I will therefore write it down.

He rose and answered me that I was on a good path all the way, and that there was plenty of lodging: that the road was safe, and that my map would be an ample guide.

"From the other side of Aurès," he said, "you will see one ridge of red rocks beyond another. Even the furthest has some scrub upon it upon this side, but from its summit you will see the desert, and on this side it is easy to climb."

The Stranger

Myself : " And how is the southern side towards the Sahara ? "

He : " It is all precipice, but from the northern side you can cast about and find a path which creeps down the end of the ridge to an oasis of palm-trees. These are very numerous and evident from the height. When you reach them you will find a large river flowing towards the desert, a great road and a railway. It is easy to return."

All this I knew already from my reading, and from my map, but I listened to him for the sake of the tones of his voice : these had a sort of laugh in them when he added that I should be glad to get back to water, to trees and to men.

Myself : " But there is, as you say and know, no danger on this road from the tribes or from beasts."

He : " No. Very little."

Myself : " What other danger can there be ? "

The Stranger

He answered that many who saw the desert learnt more than they desired to learn.

I knew very well what he meant for I had heard many men maintain that what was eternal must be changeless, and that what was changeless must be dead. And I had noted how men who had travelled widely were more simple in the Faith if they had chiefly known the sea; but if they had chiefly known the desert, more subtle and often emptied of the Faith at last: the Faith dried up out of them as the dews are dried up out of the sand on the edges of the Sahara in the brazen mornings. But these men, speaking in Christendom, had affected me little; here, so near the waste places where men cannot live, alone with such a companion, I felt afraid.

We walked along together slowly for a few paces; his sentences were shorter than my replies, and were spoken low, and full of what he and his call wisdom, but I, despair.

The Stranger

We discussed together in these brief moments the chief business of mankind. It was a power much greater than his words that put my mind into a turmoil, though his words were careful and heavy. . . . He told me that the day was better than the night. The daylight was a curtain and a cheat, but when it was gone you could see the dreadful hollow.

MYSELF : " In Sussex, which is my home, if a man were asked which was the more beneficent, he would say ' the night.' "

" In Sussex," he answered gently (as though he knew the Downs) "mists and kind airs continue the veil of the day." He said that in the desert the stars were terrible to man, and as he spoke of the endless distances I remembered the old knowledge (but this time alive with conviction) how great nations, as they advance with unbroken records and heap up experience, and test life by their own past, and grow to judge exactly the enlarging actions of men, see at last that there is no Person in destiny, and that purpose is only in themselves. Their Faiths turn to legend, and at last they enter that shrine whose God has departed and whose Idol is quite blind.

We had not talked thus for twenty minutes when we stopped at the edge of a little wood, and, as his way was not mine, he made to return. We both turned back to look at the plain below us, and the salt dull valley and the dead town: the broken columns and the long streets of Timgad, made small by the distance and all in one group together. I looked at him as he stood there and the fantastic thought half took me that he had known the city while it was yet loud with men. When he had left me the oppression of his awful intensity and of his fixed unnatural reason began to fade. I saw him go into a secchia; I saw him again upon the further side swinging powerfully down the slope. He crossed another fold of land,

The Walk to the Desert

he showed upon the crest beyond, and after that I did not see him again.

Then I turned and went up into Atlas, and as I went I was in two minds, but at last tradition conquered and I was safe in my own steadfast instincts, settling back as settles back with shorter and shorter oscillations some balanced rock which violence has disturbed. The vast shoulder of Aurès seemed worthy indeed of awe, but not of terror. I made a companion of the snow, and I was glad to remember how many living things moved under the forest trees.

So I continued for three days seeing many things, and drawing them till I came to the south side where the streams go down to be lost at last in the sand, and till I saw before me the sandstone ridge red and bare, and from its summit looked out upon a changing landscape, which dried and flattened and became the true desert where miles and miles away a line quite hard and level marked the

The Sight of the Desert

extreme horizon. On this summit I lay in the shelter of a rock (for it was bitterly cold and a violent wind blew off the snows of Aurès) and looked a long time southward upon the country which is the prison-wall of our race.

The man near Timgad had said truly that the end of the Empire, the division and the boundary, was abrupt.

A precipice falls sharply right against the midday sun ; it is built up of those red rocks whose colour adds so much to the evil silence of the Sahara, and the ridge-top of this precipice is here a sharp dividing-line between living and desert land. Africa the province, the Maghreb full of towns and men, ends in a coast, as it were, against this blinding ocean of sand. You look down from its cliffs over a vast space much more inhuman than the sea. Behind the traveller stretches all the table-land he has traversed, bare indeed and strange to a northerner, but very habit-

The View of the Desert

able and sown with large cities, living and dead. There are behind him trees, many animals and rain : all the diversity of a true climate and a long-cultivated soil. Before him are sharp reefs of stone, unweathered, without moss, and with harsh unrounded corners split by the furnace-days and the dreadful frosts of the desert. The rocks emphasise the wild desert as reefs do the wild of the sea : they rise out of sand that blows and shifts under the wind.

On this day, as I took my first long look at the Sahara, Aurès and the plateau beyond were all piled up with dark clouds, and one could see showers sweeping like shadowy curtains over the distant forests to the northward ; but southward over the desert there was a sky like a cup of blue steel, and a dazzling sunlight that made more desperate the desperate iciness of the gale. When I could tolerate the cold no longer I began to pick my way carefully downward.

The Oasis

I could not find any path such as the man at Timgad had told me of, and such as my map showed, but what I had to do was clear, for down in the plain below me a long line of palms marked an oasis and the passage of that clear river which, as I knew, comes tumbling down from the Atlas to be lost at last in the Sahara. No feature in the unusual view below me was more characteristic than this: that green leaves were thus bunched together, rare, isolated and exceptional, as with us are waste rocks or heaths, while the wide sweep of the land, which with us is all fields and trees and boundaries, here is abandoned altogether. It was not the least part of my wonder in this new place to find myself walking as I chose over an earth that was quite barren, with no history, no obstacles, and no owner, towards a patch of human land whose grove looked as an island looks from the sea. As I neared those palms I found first the railway, and then the

The Arab Riding

strong high road which the astonishing French have driven right out here into nothingness.

I did not turn to enter the native village. I had no appetite to see more of the desert than I had seen in my view from the hill. I had then seen a limit beyond which men of my sort cannot go, and I was content to leave it to those others who will remain for ever the enemies of our Europe. I saw one on the road : a true Arab, what the French call " An Arab of the Great Tent," not what we and the Algerians are, but a rider of that race which makes one family from the Persian Gulf to the Atlantic. He was on a horse going up before me into the hills, with the snow of Aurès above him, and between us a tall palm. As I watched him and admired his stately riding, I said to myself : " This is how it will end : they shall leave us to our vineyards, our statues, and our harbour-towns, and we will leave them to their desert

THE ARAB RIDING

here beyond the hills, for it is their native

place. . . . Then we shall have reached our goal, for we shall be back where the Romans were, and the empire will be fully restored. For all things return at last to their origins, and Europe must return to hers. They must

forget our cities which they ruined, and which we are so painfully rebuilding, and we will not covet their little glaring *ksours* which they build upon crags above the desert, and which are quite white in the sun. . . . This is how it will end."

When I came to that curious cleft or gorge through which the river, the road and the railway all make their way together, one above the other, from the plateau down into the desert plain, I saw a Christian house after

The Return

so many miles and days. I went in at once, drank wine, and asked the hour of the train, for I was tired of this land. I was hurrying to get back to reasonable shrines, and to smell the sea.

"Very soon," I said to myself, "I shall come back to the coast-harbours, and I shall see again all the business of the shipping and the waves; and I shall see, rounding the pier-heads, those happy boats which seem

The Last Bargain

to be part of the mist and of the very early morning." So it was; for I came at the close of a bright day through the hills of the Tell to the sea: here was the Mediterranean, and here were all the sails. I saw again the little harbour by which I had entered Africa, and I was glad to find such a choice of ships at

the quays, ready, as it seemed, to go to all parts of the world. So I chose one that was a Spaniard, bound for Palma in Majorca, and I drove a bargain by which I was to go for next to nothing, provided I stayed on deck, and ate none of their food.

When I had driven this bargain, I bought wine, bread and meat ashore, and came back and took a place right up in the bows from

The Last Bargain

which to watch the sea. It was the afternoon when we cast off and left the harbour, and before it was quite dark we had lost the land. I lay there for many hours in the bows, and thought about my home. And as I went across the sea I recalled those roofs built for true winters, and those great fireplaces of my own land. I also thought of the thick, damp woods which begin by Tay and go on to Roncesvalles, but which north or south of these are never seen ; I remembered Europe well. There were women there (to whom I was sailing) whose eyes were clear and simple, and whose foreheads low ; I remembered that all their gestures were easy. I remembered that in the harbours men would meet me kindly ; I was to meet my own people again, and their ritual would not seem to be ritual because it would be my own, and the air would be full of bells. The ship also, going eagerly onwards dead north under the stars ; she carried me towards

The Memory of Europe

my native things, herself reaching her own country, for nothing alien to Europe could make or preserve the science that had constructed such engines and such a hull.

"In Europe, in the river-valleys," I thought, "I will rest and look back, as upon an adventure, towards my journey in this African land. I shall be free of travel. I shall be back home. I shall come again to inns and little towns. I shall see railways (of which I am very fond), and I shall hear and see nothing that the Latin Order has not made." I thought about all these things as the ship drove on.

Europe filled me as I looked out over the bows, and I saluted her though she could not see me nor I her. I considered how she had made us all, how she was our mother and our author, and how in that authority of hers and of her religion a man was free. On this account, although I had no wine (for I had drunk it long before and thrown

And her Toast

the bottle overboard), I drank in my soul to her destiny. I had just come back from the land which Europe had reconquered, and which, please God, she shall continually hold, and I said to myself, "Remain for ever."

"We pass. There is nothing in ourselves that remains. But do you remain for ever. What happens to this life of ours, which we had from you, *Salvâ Fide*, I cannot tell: save that it changes and is not taken away. They say that nations perish and that at last the race itself shall decline; it is better for us of the faith to believe that you are preserved, and that your preservation is the standing grace of this world."

It was in this watch of the early morning that I called out to her "*Esto perpetua!*" which means in her undying language: "You shall not die"; and remembering this I have determined to give my rambling book that title.

* * * * *

It Dawns

In a little while it began to be dawn; but as yet I saw no land. I saw before me a boundary of waters tumbling all about, but I did not feel alone upon that sea. I felt rather as a man feels on some lake inland, knowing well that there is governed country upon every side.

This is the way in which a man leaves Africa and comes back to the shore which Christendom has never lost.

But all the while as he goes from Africa northwards, steering for the Balearics and the harbours of Spain, he remembers that other iron boundary of the Sahara which shuts us in, and the barrier against which his journey struck and turned. The silence permits him to recall most vividly the last of the oases under Atlas upon the edge of the wild.

There, where the fresh torrent that has nourished the grove is already sinking, stag-

The End

nant and brackish, to its end, a little palm-tree lives all alone and cherishes its life. Beyond it there is nothing whatsoever but the line of the sand.

FINIS